To See But Not To See
A Case Study of Visual Agnosia

Glyn W. Humphreys

Birkbeck College, London University
Malet Street, London

M. Jane Riddoch

North East London Polytechnic
Romford Road, London

Psychology Press
a member of the Taylor & Francis group

Reprinted 1989, 1992, 1993, 1995, 1998

Psychology Press Ltd, Publishers
27 Church Road
Hove, East Sussex
BN3 2FA
UK

British Library Cataloguing in Publication Data

Humphreys, Glyn W.
    To see but not to see: A case study of visual agnosia.
    1. Visual perception 2. Eye—Diseases and defects
    3. Optics, Physiological
    I.Title II. Riddoch, M. Jane
    152.1'4 BF241

    ISBN 0-86377-065-7

Printed and bound in the UK by BPC Wheatons Ltd, Exeter

Contents

Preface

The brain can be damaged in many different ways: by a cerebral haemorrhage or by a blockage of one of the blood vessels supplying the brain; by direct impact of a missile; by tumour, etc. Brain damage of any sort may cause a whole range of symptoms, but occasionally a patient suffers from a very selective problem. One such problem is visual agnosia; difficulty in recognising common objects from vision. Now, sometimes a person will suffer blurred vision after being concussed, and the idea that vision may be affected in this way after a "bump on the head" is fairly familiar. The odd thing about agnosia is that it is not like this. In some cases, patients may be able to copy the object they are looking at, and they may describe the parts of the object in fine detail. Their vision is not blurred. Yet somehow the object does not seem to make sense any more, they are unable to decide whether it is familiar, and so can be quite unaware of what it is or what it may be used for. They will fail to "recognise" the object.

This book describes the case of a patient (John) who has a particularly "pure" form of visual agnosia. John is an interesting patient for several reasons, but most especially because his problem is so selectively confined to visual recognition, and because he has an unusual degree of insight into his own problem. Given the rarity of visual agnosia, it is encumbant upon us to provide as extensive a study of such a selectively affected patient as possible. This is the first aim of the book. In doing this, we hope to illustrate the ways in which visual recognition breaks down, and the kinds of problems this produces in everyday life.

A more particular aim of the book is to describe our study of John's

1

case, and the implications of this study for understanding the processes normally involved in visual recognition. Until recently, neurological case studies tended to describe and categorize particular patients, and then to emphasize the relations between the disturbed behaviour and the place in the brain where damage had occurred. However, more recently, a slightly different approach has developed. This new approach attempts to take theories of normal cognitive abilities—concerning, say, reading, memory or visual recognition—and to use these theories as a framework for understanding how the abilities break down following brain damage (e.g. Coltheart, Patterson & Marshall, 1980; Humphreys & Riddoch, in press/a). By taking an account of normal performance as a starting point, researchers hope to provide a richer explanation of the problems experienced by patients, since any problems can be related to the processes that support normal behaviour. An additional hope is that such patients will also help to formulate and refine theories of normal behaviour, particularly where the problem experienced by the patient reflects selective damage to one process. The role of that process in different behaviours may then be better understood. This new approach is termed "cognitive neuropsychology".

The case study of John conforms to what might be thought to be a cognitive neuropsychological approach. We begin with a brief discussion of previous cases of agnosia, and an outline of evidence concerning the way in which visual recognition appears to be implemented in the brain (Chapter 1). Chapter 2 then provides a description of John's recognition problem, in his own words and those of his wife, Iris. Our hope is that these descriptions give informal background information on the nature of the problem, and illustrate the many problems that arise when visual recognition falters. From such descriptions we can learn something about the tremendous complexity of visual recognition, about whose component processes we are usually completely unaware. Following these initial chapters, we outline the broad details of our case study. Since it is a cognitive neuropsychological approach, taking an account of normal visual recognition as its starting point, we first consider the processes normally involved in visual recognition, using evidence drawn from both experimental psychology and computer vision (Chapter 3). Some of the questions which remain to be answered, and which will be addressed by John's case, are outlined. Chapters 4, 5 and 6 then describe our case study. Chapter 4 deals with John's visual recognition problems. Chapter 5 deals with some of the ancillary problems John encounters in everyday life (problems with finding his way, with recognising people and with reading), and Chapter 6 presents some conclusions concerning both theories of normal visual recognition and recognition disorders. Finally, Chapter 7 gives an outline, in Iris's words, of how John's life has progressed since he suffered the stroke which caused his agnosia.

The book is intended for all those interested in the scientific understanding of the mind, and particularly for those interested in understanding vision. The case study is presented in descriptive terms, but for those interested in the details of the specific tests used, reference should be made to a series of papers which have been reported on John's case (in these papers John is referred to by his initials, H. J. A.) These papers are as follows: Bromley et al., 1986; Humphreys & Riddoch, 1984; Humphreys, Riddoch, & Quinlan, 1985; Riddoch & Humphreys, 1986; Riddoch & Humphreys, in press/a.

Any work of this nature is a collaborative venture, and there are many people who have contributed to the research. Drs Mary Hill and John Patten, of Farnham Road Hospital, Guildford, initially gave us access to John. Recordings of John's visual fields were undertaken by Professor Geoffrey Arden, of the Institute of Ophthalmology, and by the Ophthalmology Department of King's College Hospital, London. Professor Arden also conducted EEG recordings. Drs Chris Kennard and Trevor Crawford, of the London Hospital, kindly undertook the recordings of John's eye movements. Those who have helped in collecting experimental data and in forming our ideas about John's recognition problem include Jane Bromley, Max Coltheart, Kate Hilliar, Atapha Javadnia, Cathy Price, Philip Quinlan, Susan Rickard, Keith Ruddock and Barbara Wilson. Chris Kennard, Cathy Price and Keith Ruddock also kindly helped by reading through earlier drafts of the book, and Rohays Perry and Patricia Simpson provided much-needed editorial guidance. Freddie Elliott provided all the glossy figures. Alan Cowey, John Frisby, Richard Gregory, Bela Julesz, Stephen Palmer, Graham Ratcliff and Irvin Rock all gave their permission to use their figures, and the editor of the *Journal of Neurology, Neurosurgery and Psychiatry* also kindly gave us permission to quote sections from case studies in articles published in that journal. Finally, we are grateful to both Cathy Price and Philip Quinlan for "holding the fort" while the book was being written.

The work covered in the book has been supported by grants from various sources. For the past five years, Glyn Humphreys's work on visual object recognition has been supported by the Social and Economic Research Council of Great Britain. In addition, our joint work has been funded by the Chest, Heart and Stroke Association and by the Medical Research Council of Great Britain, and we have received travel support from the London University Research Fund. Without such support, the work would not have been possible.

The writing of the book depended greatly on the support and forebearance of our family, and in particular of our children, Iain, Alec and Kate.

Finally, the whole project could not have proceeded without the kindness and continuing interest of John and Iris, who have participated uncomplainingly in hours of tedious tests, and who, beyond everything else, have made the road to discovery such a pleasure. It is to them, with thanks, that this book is dedicated.

1 Visual Object Recognition and its Disorders

We are surrounded by objects. Our lives are spent identifying, classifying, using and judging objects. Objects are tools, shelter, weapons; they are food; they are things precious, beautiful, boring, frightening, lovable ... almost everything we know. We are so used to objects, to seeing them wherever we look, that is quite difficult to realise that they present any problem.

(Gregory, 1970; p. 11)

INTRODUCTION

The term "visual object recognition" refers to our ability to apprehend the meaning of objects, our prior associations with them, and their uses, from vision. Normally, visual object recognition occurs at a glance, with such apparently effortless alacrity that it is indeed difficult to realise the complexity of the processes involved, or that understanding how we recognise objects should be such a problem. Most people feel that the visual world is simply given to them from the information relayed to the brain from the eyes, and that no more by way of explanation is needed. Yet such is the complexity of the processes involved that, even after more than a century of careful investigation, our knowledge of visual recognition and of how it is implemented in the brain remains all too incomplete. We are still some way from achieving the kind of detailed knowledge that would, for instance, allow us to build a machine to see and recognise objects in the manner that we do. What is certainly true is that the end product of visual recognition, our ability to act on and to negotiate the visual world appropriately, tells us little about the complex processes behind its production.

Various lines of investigation might be taken towards understanding how we recognise objects. For instance, one might attempt to build a machine capable of making the same responses as ourselves to visual input (such as identifying an object). In doing this, one would hope to glean some of the processes which might have to be involved in interpreting that input, irrespective of whether the interpretation is done by a human or a machine. Another approach might be to study the efficiency with which we recognise different types of objects under contrasting viewing conditions. For instance, one might present objects very briefly to normal observers and look at the kinds of misidentification errors they make. In doing this, one might hope to learn about the beginnings of the perceptual process (about which kind of information is picked up first, and so on). Thus when observers misidentify a drawing of a donkey as a dog, for example, one might conclude that they have picked up information about the general shape of the picture rather than its detailed features. It would then follow that general shape information is picked up "early on" in perceptual processing. A third approach is to study the selective losses of visual function which can occur after damage to the visual system, and in particular after damage to the brain. The hope is that, in such cases, we are given a privileged view of how the normal system operates in isolation from the damaged component(s). We may thus learn something about the nature of the various functions by examining how their loss affects recognition.

This book serves to illustrate this third approach. In it we document the case of a patient who, due to a stroke, suffered highly selective brain damage affecting only his visual recognition ability. The patient, John, is remarkable in many respects. From a purely academic point of view his case is of great interest because the effects of the brain damage have been so selective, disrupting only certain aspects of visual recognition. John's case may therefore illuminate some of the processes in vision, and the ways in which these processes are organised in the brain. More generally, his case demonstrates just how devastating the selective loss of abilities such as visual object recognition can be, and yet how people adapt to cope with such losses. We hope the lessons to be learned will not be solely academic.

WHAT IS VISUAL AGNOSIA?

Before we can begin to understand the kinds of problems John encounters when trying to recognise objects, and why these problems might arise, we need to put his case in the context of previous studies of similar cases. This will give us a framework within which we can understand his recognition disorder.

Patients who, following brain damage, have problems in recognising formerly familiar objects from sight are said to suffer *visual agnosia*. Somebody with this disorder is able to "see" objects; that is, they may be able to describe the parts of an object or they may be able to copy a picture of it, but they have no idea what the object is or how it might be used. What makes the condition even more puzzling is that if the patient is allowed to hold and to feel the object, he or she is often able to identify it. Cases of visual agnosia are extremely rare, although they have been documented since the late nineteenth century. Even rarer still are detailed analyses of what such cases may tell us about how visual recognition normally works. One early account of visual agnosia is that of Charcot (1883). He described the case of a well-educated man, known for a remarkable visual memory, who, as a result of a stroke, suddenly lost the ability to recognise and visualise places, colours, forms, and human faces. He no longer recognised familiar aquaintances (not even his wife and children), and he no longer recognised his own face. Charcot describes an occasion when this patient was standing in the passage of a public place and found that his way was blocked. He was about to excuse himself to the man who stood in front of him when he realised it was only his own reflection in a mirror.

Around the same time, a physiologist, Hermann Munk, who was involved in the experimental study of the functions of the various parts of the brain, removed the posterior parts of the brain (the occipital lobes) in a dog and found that the dog subsequently behaved in a similar way to the patient described by Charcot (Munk, 1881). The dog was found to have no abnormality of hearing, smell, taste, movement or sensation. It moved about quite normally both indoors and in the garden and could apparently still "see" objects to the extent that it would walk around those placed in its way; it would neither walk into them nor trip over them. However, the dog no longer appeared to recognise the people that it had known well in the past and it would ignore other dogs. It no longer appeared to recognise its food and water bowls and would go around them as if they were obstacles that had been placed in its path (though it would respond to the food if near enough to smell it). The sight of the whip which, in the past, would drive the dog into the corner, no longer frightened it at all. The dog had also been trained to present a paw in response to a hand waved in front of its eyes; now, however much a hand was waved, the dog would ignore it. Unlike human subjects with visual-object agnosia, Munk's dog did not suffer its disorder for long. Within a few weeks it could once again recognise its master and other dogs and would respond in a normal fashion to them.

Charcot and Munk accounted for the disorder which had occurred in both man and dog in an essentially similar way. Munk devised the term "mind-blindness", by which he meant that there was a loss of visual ideas and visual memories, so there was no longer an ability to recognise what was seen. However, it was accepted that both man and dog could see because they could walk about and negotiate obstacles quite apropriately.

VISUAL RECOGNITION AND THE BRAIN

Given the existence of patients with such a selective problem in visually recognising objects, a number of questions spring to mind—such as: How could damage to the brain generate such a problem? To answer such questions, we need to consider some points about the nature of brain function and organisation.

The brain is a complex structure, containing about 100,000,000,000 cells or neurons. It is divided into different sections, which have different evolutionary histories and which serve different purposes. For instance, the top part of the brain, termed the cerebrum, is thought to be concerned with our higher mental processes. The cerebrum sits above other structures which are, in evolutionary terms, rather older, such as the thalamus (a kind of sensory relay station) and the cerebellum (concerned with the co-ordination of voluntary movement, balance etc.). The cerebrum itself is divided down the middle into two cerebral hemispheres, with communication between the hemispheres made possible by a connecting structure termed the corpus callosum. The surface layer of neurons within each hemisphere is called the cerebral cortex, which folds over and under itself many times, rather like a very crumpled sheet. Enclosed beneath the cortex is the so-called "white" matter, consisting of masses of nerve fibres which relay messages within the brain and between the brain and the body. These structures are illustrated in Fig. 1.1.

The way in which messages are relayed from the eyes to the brain is not as straightforward as one might initially think. Messages are passed from each eye along an optic nerve. The optic nerves join at the optic chiasm, where some fibres from each nerve cross over and connect to the cerebral hemisphere on the opposite side. By means of this partial crossing-over of nerve fibres, fibres to the left of the central part of both retinae project back to the left cerebral hemisphere, and fibres to the right of the centres of the retinae project to the right hemisphere. Now, due to the laws of optics, all stimuli to the right of the line of sight (or fixation) will fall on the left halves of both retinae, while stimuli to the left of fixation fall on the right halves of both retinae, as illustrated in Fig. 1.2. This means that

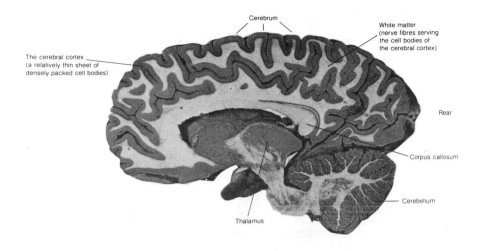

FIG. 1.1. The human brain, sliced from front to rear through the right cerebral hemisphere (from Frisby, 1979).

stimuli to the left of fixation project information directly to the right cerebral hemisphere, whilst stimuli to the right of fixation project directly to the left hemisphere (by way of the lateral geniculate nucleus and the optic radiations; see Fig. 1.2). The optic radiations are the final structures involved in relaying messages to the cortex, and they project primarily to what is termed the striate cortex, or visual area 1 (Vl), within the occipital lobe at the posterior end of the brain (see Fig. 1.3). Fibres from the striate cortex then project forward in the brain to adjacent regions in the prestriate cortex (so called because this area of cortex lies just in front of the striate cortex). In addition to this primary visual pathway, messages are relayed directly from both retinae to a mid-brain structure termed the superior colliculus (Fig. 1.2). The superior colliculus, unlike the striate cortex, does not appear to be directly involved in visual recognition; rather it appears to be involved in the way in which we attend to visual events, and particularly in the guidance of the eyes to novel stimuli.

Damage to various parts of the visual pathway can produce characteristic "visual field defects", where regions of the visual field are rendered effectively blind to light (see Fig. 1.2). One might thus initially think that visual agnosia, the selective problem in recognising objects visually, is due to a field defect of this sort. However, this does not appear to be the case. These field defects do not usually cause recognition problems in their own right since vision remains intact in the remaining areas of the field. Providing that an object falls within those remaining areas, it will be recognised.

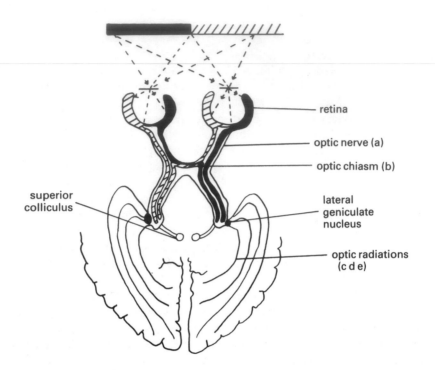

FIG. 1.2.   The visual pathways to the brain. Damage to the different sites shown produces the following visual field defects (in all cases, lesions of the same sites on the left side of the brain will produce equivalent field defects, but in the right rather than the left visual field):

	Left eye	Right eye
Lesion of the right optic nerve (a):	○	●
Lesion of the optic chiasm (b):	◑	◐
Complete lesion of the optic radiations projecting to the right hemisphere (c):	◑	◑
Lesion to the upper radiations projecting to the right hemisphere (d):	◕	◕
Lesion to the lower radiations projecting to the right hemisphere (e):	◔	◔

One of the most significant advances in understanding the way in which visual recognition is implemented in the brain came about in the early 1960s with the work of two physiologists, David Hubel and Torsten Wiesel. Hubel and Wiesel (e.g., 1962, 1968) conducted a series of studies in which they recorded the response's of single cells in the striate cortex of the cat to various stimuli projected to different parts of the retina. They found that the cells demonstrated distinct preferences for specific stimuli, being greatly excited by some stimuli and not at all by others. Of special interest was the finding that some cells responded strongly to the edges of stimuli and to light or dark bars at particular orientations. Also, different cells preferred edges in different orientations and the responses of these cells waxed and waned depending on how close the orientation of the actual edge was to the orientation preferred by the cell. Further, each cell was associated with a particular part of the retina, so that information concerning the location of each edge in space was pre-served. By preserving location information, the cells in the striate cortex may be said to contain a "map" of the retina. These cells have commonly been labelled "feature detectors", since they were initially thought to be capable, individually, of signalling the presence of a particular kind of edge in any visual stimulus. It turns out that such a view is almost certainly wrong, for reasons we discuss in more detail in Chapter 3. Nevertheless, the discovery of these cells did provide some inkling of the initial coding processes upon which visual recognition is based, indicating that recognition initially involves coding the edges and contours of objects. However, recognition clearly cannot be based on this coding alone, since we cannot recognise objects from single edges. Recognition must involve considerable elaboration of the edge and bar information coded in the primary visual cortex, area V1.

Since Hubel and Wiesel's pioneering work, a good deal of research has been devoted to generating a picture of the stimulus preferences of the cells in the cortex concerned with visual processing. The evidence points clearly to the involvement of many brain areas in the processing of a given object. For instance, researchers have documented eight different cortical areas concerned with vision in the owl monkey (e.g., Weller & Kaas, 1985), eleven in the macaque monkey (e.g., Van Essen, 1985) and thirteen in the cat (e.g., Tusa, Palmer & Rosenquist, 1975); and we may presume that the human visual system is at least as complex as that of the monkey or the cat. These different visual areas extend from the striate cortex (V1) into the pre-striate cortex in the occipital lobe, and also further forward into the parietal lobes (at the top of the brain) and temporal lobes (at the side of the brain; see Fig. 1.3). The areas can be identified because they contain, amongst other things, differing cell types and complete or partial replica-tions of the map of the retina (i.e., some seem to mirror the organisation of the cells in the retina, whereas others are only related to some of the cells of the retina). We might then ask what the need is for this multitude of visual areas, many of which contain cells tuned to the same area of the retina as cells in other visual areas. One likely answer is that these different areas are the sites of increasingly refined processing of visual images. Further, there are different connections from area V1, the source of the major projection from the retina, to a number of other visual areas (see, for example, the work of Zeki, 1978). These different connections allow the possibility that the further processing of images is conducted simultaneously in the various visual areas, with each area doing a different job.

The main sets of connections from V1 go either to the parietal or to the temporal lobe, and it has been suggested that these two secondary pathways serve different purposes (see Ungerleider, 1985): the parietal pathway being concerned with coding the location, movement and spatial relations between stimuli, the temporal pathway with the actual recognition of the stimuli. Support for this suggestion, and also for the further differentiation of areas within the parietal and temporal pathways, comes from more recent studies using single-cell recording techniques. For instance, the temporal pathway contains, along with other areas, two areas termed V2 and V4 (Fig. 1.3). Some cells in V2 respond specifically to differences in the positions of stimuli in the images from the left and right eyes (Fischer & Poggio, 1979). These differences, termed "binocular disparities", are one of the main cues we use to help us judge whether objects are at different distances from us (for more detail on this, see Chapter 4). Cells in V4, on the other hand, respond selectively to different colours (Zeki, 1980). These differing preferences tempt us to conclude that these two areas code different visual properties, with V2 implicated in perceiving depth and V4 in perceiving colour (see Cowey, 1979). Further, the pathway from V1 to the parietal lobe includes an area termed "MT" (Fig. 1.3), where the cells respond differentially to stimuli moving at

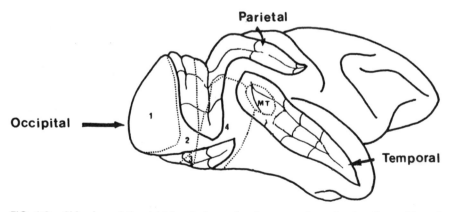

FIG. 1.3. Side-view of the right hemisphere of a rhesus monkey, showing the position of various visual areas. The front of the brain is on the right. Four of the major convolutions in the brain have been "opened out" to reveal their recesses. The numbers and initials refer to different identified visual areas (modified from Cowey, 1985). Visual areas which are not mentioned in the text are not marked.

different speeds and in different directions (Zeki, 1974). We might thus suggest that area MT is involved in the perception of movement. Interestingly, these three areas (V2, V4 and MT) appear to have the property of exclusivity; cells in V2 and V4 will not respond to movement only and cells in MT may show little reaction to colour or disparity information.

The picture that emerges is of different brain areas analysing different types of visual information. In particular, there seem to be different areas concerned with perceiving binocular disparities, colour, and movement (areas V2, V4 and MT respectively). What follows from this is that selective damage to these brain areas might affect only those processes they are individually concerned with.

A perusal of the neurological literature reveals many instances of remarkable and specific disorders of various aspects of vision, visual agnosia being only one member of a whole family of disorders. The relations between such disorders and the kinds of studies of brain organisation we have discussed here can be illustrated by considering cases of selective disturbance to the processes we have already highlighted: namely, stereoscopic depth perception, colour perception, and movement.

The most straightforward of these cases concern stereoscopic depth perception and movement perception. Danta, Hilton and O'Boyle (1978) have argued that selective disorders of stereoscopic depth perception are not uncommon following damage to the prestriate cortex in man, though such disorders may often remain undetected because the patients can retain good monocular vision, and intact visual recognition. Effectively, such patients may act as people do after losing an eye; their depth perception may suffer, but they otherwise function normally.

More dramatic is the case documented by Zihl, von Cramon and Mai (1983), of a patient who had sustained a lesion to the prestriate cortex in both cerebral hemispheres (i.e., the lesion was *bilateral*). This patient had a strange disorder in that she no longer had any impression of continuous movement. For instance, when pouring tea into a cup, the moving liquid appeared frozen, like a glacier; she would then find it difficult to know when to stop pouring because she could not see the liquid rising; she also found it difficult to follow dialogues because she could not see the movements of the face; and she found it difficult to cross the road because cars appeared suddenly, in different places, rather than appearing to move continuously. The patient was also poor at discriminating between moving and stationary objects that appeared in her central vision. However, as might be expected from our argument concerning the functional specialization of visual processing in the brain, the patient could see stationary forms, colour, and depth quite normally. This case is consistent with the idea that the brain area concerned with motion perception is separate from those concerned with depth, colour, and static form perception, and so it is liable to selective brain damage.

Colour vision can be affected by brain damage in various ways, and in the most startling cases it can be lost altogether. This condition is called "cerebral achromatopsia" (meaning the absence of colour vision due to damage to the cerebral cortex), and it is again linked to damage to the prestriate cortex (Meadows, 1974). Patients with cerebral achromatopsia report that the world appears in various shades of grey, and their ability to carry out any tasks involving colour discrimination is often very poor. Interestingly, the disorder is completely unrelated to the more usual types of "colour-blindness", which are due to the absence of certain pigments in the retina. Cerebral achromatopsic patients can be shown to have completely intact retinal mechanisms for processing colour (Mollon, Newcombe, Polden & Ratcliff, 1980), but it is as if they simply cannot interpret that information in the way that we normally do when we "see" colour. Other visual functions, such as the ability to achieve a sharp image (visual acuity) and the ability to see movement, may be intact. However, in cerebral achromatopsia the colour perception disorder is associated with disorders of visual recognition, in that the patients are often also poor at recognising complex visual stimuli, such as faces (Meadows, 1974). Now, since we can interpret black and white images quite easily (on the television or in photographs), we can presume that the loss of colour vision itself is not the cause of such recognition problems. Thus the association between disorders of colour perception and visual recognition in these cases must occur for other reasons. For instance, it might be that the brain area specializing in colour perception is anatomically close to that specializing in visual recognition; since the natural causes of brain damage in man (such as stroke or tumour) are no respecters of functional boundaries in the brain, any damage to the colour area is also likely to affect the visual recognition area. Alternatively, it might be that the area specializing in colour perception also plays some crucial role in visual recognition (i.e., it may be concerned with form processing as well as colour perception), in which case damage to the colour area will affect both colour perception and visual recognition.

This brief discussion illustrates how information from cases of selective losses of visual function can converge with that from single-cell studies to give us a richer picture of the way in which visual recognition happens in the brain. But the picture remains incomplete. One problem concerns whether the areas allocated specific functions from single-cell recording work (Fig. 1.3) are really those damaged when losses of the functions are recorded in man. Often the anatomical information about cases of brain damage in man is insufficient to enable a direct linkage to be made with the single-cell recording studies. For instance, cerebral achromatopsia is one disorder that is closely linked with a lesion site, because it is associated with a visual field defect that helps to pin-point the site of the lesion. This field defect involves the upper regions of both the left and right visual fields (and is termed a "superior altitudinal field defect"; see Meadows, 1974). A defect to both the left and right fields suggests that there is a lesion to both cerebral hemispheres (see Fig. 1.2), and one which affects only the upper parts of the fields suggests a lesion in the region of the lower secondary pathway from the visual area in the occipital lobe to the temporal lobe. Thus cerebral achromatopsia is associated with a bilateral lesion in an area of the prestriate cortex extending to the temporal lobe. From the single-cell recording work we know that this temporal lobe pathway contains area V4, identified as important to colour perception in the monkey; but it remains an open question as to whether V4 alone is damaged in such cases. Such questions may come to be answered with improvements to our techniques of recording the site and extent of brain damage.

An even more serious problem concerns visual recognition. This is because the single-cell recording work as yet provides no clear indication of how outputs from the primitive feature-processing cells identified by Hubel and Wiesel are combined to enable whole forms to be recognised, rather than single lines or edges. This is despite the fact that some recent single-cell recording studies have produced quite impressive evidence, indicating that cells towards the front end of the temporal lobe of the monkey show preferences for particular faces in particular orientations (e.g., Perret et al., 1985). This finding is consistent with the idea that the temporal lobe projection mediates visual recognition. But, it throws little light on how the information supplied by the edge-processing units in area V1 comes to be organised so that other cells, far along the processing chain, are excited by information as specific as a familiar face seen at one particular angle. This highlights what is probably the fundamental weakness of such approaches, which concern solely the correlation between visual recognition and brain activity: the simple documenting of correlations fails to tell us about the processes involved, or why such processes are necessary. For instance, we need to know *why* it is useful to code information in images about lines and edges at particular orientations, and how such information is combined to give us accurate information about whole objects. Such questions are addressed by considering the processes upon which visual recognition is based, and how these processes might be disturbed by brain damage.

DIFFERENT TYPES OF AGNOSIA

In the preceding discussion, we distinguished between different visual functions (concerning stereoscopic depth, colour, and movement perception), and we tried to show how lesions to particular parts of the brain can selectively impair the different functions. By applying similar ideas to visual agnosia, we might learn something about the functions and the brain areas involved in visual recognition. A relevant question here is whether visual recognition is a single process, or whether it is itself composed of various, rather separate functions. For instance, it could be that patients have problems recognising objects for quite different reasons, so that there exist different *types* of agnosia. This point is clearly important if we are to infer anything about the processes involved in visual recognition from agnosia.

It is certainly true that the performance of agnosic patients on different tasks is inconsistent. Not only do different patients perform differently on different tasks, but one patient may perform differently on the same task presented on two separate occasions. The first of these points led Lissauer (1890) to propose that there might be two different kinds of agnosia: "apperceptive visual agnosia" and "associative visual agnosia". In the first sort, apperceptive visual agnosia, the perceptual abilities that enable us to tell one shape from another are thought to be disrupted. The patient is thus unable to recognise that two forms such as a square and a rectangle are the same or different, and is unable to copy pictures of objects. Well-documented cases of this sort of disorder are rare, and those cases which have been documented are often limited by the lack of quantitative investigation of the patient's perceptual abilities. Nevertheless, patients who may be said to fall into this general category have been documented by Adler (1944, 1950), Benson and Greenberg (1969), and Campion (in press; Campion & Latto, 1985). One interesting point about these patients is that they all suffered brain damage due to carbon monoxide poisoning.

Benson and Greenberg's patient, a soldier, was able to identify colours, appreciate changes in light intensity and indicate the direction in which an object was moving. These intact abilities were taken to indicate intact sensations. However, the patient could not match an object with a picture of the same object, nor could he match simple shapes. Attempts to copy letters or items were quite bizarre as is shown in Figs. 1.4, 1.5, and 1.6.

The same problem has been described in the case of Adler's patient (Adler, 1944; 1950). When the patient was asked why she found copying so difficult, she replied: "When it is curved I should trace round. But I see other parts and I lose myself. Then I do not see the beginning any more." With such a seemingly profound disorder, it becomes difficult to imagine how such a person would be able to find their way about the world. Strangely though, it does not appear to present such a great problem. Benson and Greenberg state that their patient "appeared attentive to his surroundings and could navigate corridors successfully in his wheelchair." Adler was also curious as to how her patient could manage beyond the sheltered environs of the hospital. Her patient, whilst having some difficulties, was able to manage surprisingly well:

> At home ... she confused the silver on the table. When getting dressed she had difficulties, confusing her underwear with her blouse and not getting her arms into the right sleeves. After the first three months, these errors did not recur. Twice she fell down the steps while descending, and she comments

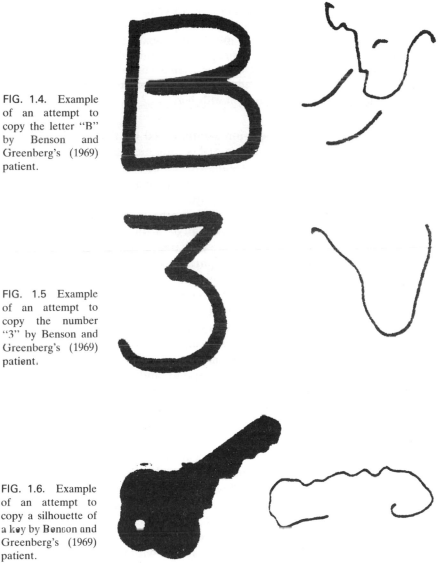

FIG. 1.4. Example of an attempt to copy the letter "B" by Benson and Greenberg's (1969) patient.

FIG. 1.5 Example of an attempt to copy the number "3" by Benson and Greenberg's (1969) patient.

FIG. 1.6. Example of an attempt to copy a silhouette of a key by Benson and Greenberg's (1969) patient.

that she is likely to overlook steps. She has no difficulty in walking up .... The patient's reading difficulties prevent her from cooking, since she confuses the different ingredients marked by labels. When sewing, she misplaces the stitches and has therefore given it up after several attempts. She takes care of her laundry but the result is poor because she misses soiled parts. She is able to iron material of simple geometric forms such as handkerchiefs and towels, but with more complicated patterns she misses parts. For instance ... she did not iron the collar on her blouse. When using the vacuum cleaner she omits sections of the rug. When crossing busy street intersections she frequently overlooks approaching cars because she perceives only part of the whole situation. Consequently, she avoids such places, unless they are protected by traffic lights. Apart from these obvious difficulties and her slowness, which is caused by her way of visual recognition, neither her family nor her friends notice any change in the patient's personality. She shows adequate affect and interest and it is possible to conduct an ordinary conversation with her.

In such cases, visual recognition seems based on the identification of visual cues which provide a more-or-less unique definition of a given object; there seems to be little assimilation of what we might think of as the "whole" object. Also, once a conspicuous feature of the object is identified, the patient may form a hypothesis and attempt to see whether the rest of the picture fits in with this hypothesis. For example, Adler's patient named a green toy battleship as first "a fountain pen", second "a green knife", and third "a boat". She described the process of identification thus: "At first I saw the front part. It looked like a fountain pen because it was shaped like a fountain pen. Then it looked like a knife because it was so sharp, but I thought it could not be a knife because it was green. Then I saw the spokes and that it was shaped like a boat, like in a movie where I'd seen boats. It had too many spokes to be a knife or a fountain pen." Campion (in press) also remarks on the particular difficulties experienced by this sort of patient and writes: "All identifications were difficult ... he often hesitated and was uncertain of the correctness of his responses ... both observation of his own performance and his own reports of what he was doing made it clear that he was using partial cues to make inferences about the identity of the items."

Lissaur's second form of visual agnosia, associative visual agnosia, differs from apperceptive visual agnosia in that the patient is thought to perceive things very well; such patients may show no difficulty following the outside line of a figure and they are able to copy and match figures (e.g., Albert, Reches, & Silverberg, 1975; Gomori & Hawryluk, 1984; Macrae & Trolle, 1956; Pallis, 1955). However, they then appear unable to interpret the meaning of the form; to relate a rectangular shape, for example, to a book, box or tray. Like patients with apperceptive agnosia, at least some patients with associative agnosia try to identify parts of a picture before attempting to identify the "whole". Wapner, Judd, and Gardner (1978) describe the case of an amateur artist who suffered from associative agnosia as a result of a stroke. When asked how he set about identifying a picture he said: "I have to use my mind to interpret what I am seeing. My eyes used to do that." When shown a drawing of two giraffes he gave the following description: "The way this comes down, this could be an animal, four legs and a tail . . . a long neck comes up, an awfully long neck . . . here's a head because here's an eye . . . two crude drawings of some kinds of animals . . . not a mouse God knows . . . what would have such an extraordinary long neck? . . . a giraffe."

AGNOSIA AND ITS SCEPTICS

It seems, then, that we can distinguish between different types of visual agnosia, and that patients can have problems in visual recognition for rather different reasons. It seems clear that we need to understand the nature of a patient's problem in some detail if our conclusions are to be relevant to accounts of normal vision.

However, we should also note that not all researchers have been convinced of the relevance of visual agnosia for understanding visual recognition. There are probably several reasons for the scepticism sometimes encountered, at least one being the rarity of the disorder. This rarity can be explained on anatomical grounds. The recognition disorder a patient suffers may well depend on the type and extent of any brain lesion. In at least some cases, agnosia is linked to bilateral brain damage (i.e., damage to both the left and right cerebral hemispheres) to regions bordering the occipital and temporal lobes (to the rear of the brain; e.g., Mack & Boller, 1977; Ratcliff & Newcombe, 1982). The posterior parts of the brain, especially the occipital lobes, are supplied by two posterior cerebral arteries, which come from a common basilar artery. It is therefore possible that obstruction to the blood supply to that part of the brain could produce bilateral brain damage (e.g., damage which occurs to both occipital lobes simultaneously). However, any moderate to large bilateral lesion produced in this way is likely to damage major portions of the striate cortex (V1) and so render the patient blind to visual forms. Thus agnosia must be due to a relatively small lesion of this type. Further, vascular damage tends to occur more frequently with the middle rather than the posterior cerebral arteries, because the middle cerebral arteries follow a more convoluted course (indeed, Charcot termed one of the minor arteries running off the middle cerebral artery the "artery of cerebral haemorrhage"). So posterior brain damage of this sort tends in any case to be infrequent. A final factor relates to brain injury from missiles. Many significant advances to our understanding of how brain injury impairs human performance have come through studying the effects of wartime missile wounds (which sometimes cause very specific damage; e.g., Holmes, 1918; Riddoch, 1917). Unfortunately, penetrating missile wounds which occur low enough in the brain to affect the regions bordering the occipital and temporal lobes are also likely to cause death by damaging vital brain-stem structures (controlling respiratory and cardiac functions). Consequently, agnosia tends to be rare amongst the missile-wounded population.

Because agnosia is uncommon, few clinicians have dealt with agnosic patients. Perhaps for this reason, the very existence of agnosia as a distinct clinical syndrome has been doubted (Bender & Feldman, 1972). Others have argued that the visual recognition disorder in visual agnosic patients is a secondary consequence of a residual deficit in visual sensation, perhaps occurring in combination with decreased intellectual function or dementia. Such a view would hold that a primary deficit in the process of visual recognition itself does not occur.

Perhaps the strongest proponent of such a view was a German neurologist, Eberhard Bay. At a conference for neurologists and psychiatrists in Badenweiler (South West Germany) in 1950, he argued most vehemently that patients with visual agnosia had not been tested rigorously enough. He claimed that if they had been so tested, basic defects in visual sensation would be demonstrated which could account for their recognition problems. Other neurologists were quick to concur with this view. Critchley (1964) remarked "never does a patient claim that he is seeing the form clearly—rather, his responses are like those of a normal person viewing an object which is partially occluded or flashed but for a few milliseconds. He seems involved in a guessing game, in making deductions about the object based on a partial and imperfect sampling of the field". Similar ideas are also reflected in the writings of earlier theorists. Pavlov (1927) suggested of Munk's dog experiments that the classical formula "the dog sees but does not understand" should be replaced with "the dog understands but does not see sufficiently well". Bay's challenge, that patients with visual agnosia had not been tested sufficiently well, was taken seriously by other workers in the field and a number of patients ran the gauntlet of a series of extensive visual tests that had been proposed by Bay. Bay himself was able to demonstrate impaired sensation in the case of one man with visual agnosia (Bay, 1953). For instance, Bay found that for this patient a light presented to a fixed part of the visual field faded abnormally rapidly. Bay argued that because the functional capacity of the central parts of the retina is greater than that of the peripheral regions, information in the periphery would fade more rapidly, producing a kind of tunnel vision. Because of this tunnel vision, the patient may be unable to "see" things as a whole. However, other investigators were unable to establish any clear relationship between such disorders of sensation and recognition deficits in patients. For example, Ettlinger and Wyke (1961) found some mild impairments of elementary visual processes in their patient but did not feel that these were sufficient to account for the patient's difficulties in recognition. A similar claim is made by Newcombe and Ratcliff (1975) of their visual agnosic patient.

Eberhard Bay did not only feel that patients with visual agnosia had impaired basic visual processes, he also felt that they were demented in some way. This explanation would not seem unreasonable to a member of the general public whose beloved relative started to demonstrate the strange symptoms associated with visual agnosia. This can be illustrated by a case of Nielsen's (1946). She was a right-handed woman who, as the result of a stroke, developed problems in recognising objects by sight and in finding her way. The bizarre symptoms led her family to assume that the patient had a mental disturbance and they attempted to have her committed as insane.

> The patient could not feed herself during the last four months of life. The husband stated that she did not recognise the difference between food on her plate and her glass of milk, nor could she tell what to take with her fork or her spoon. He knew she was not blind because she avoided knocking things over and reached correctly with her hands, she merely acted as though she did not recognise what she saw. When visitors came, she was more lively and entered into conversation, but her disability in finding her way about the house continued and friends became convinced that she was peculiar mentally.

Bay's claim was, however, based on stronger evidence. He had been asked to see the patient described by Goldstein and Gelb (Goldstein & Gelb, 1918). This patient had been wounded by shrapnel in the First World War which had resulted in a marked difficulty in the ability to recognise objects. On the basis of their study of this patient, Goldstein and Gelb had developed a novel view of visual agnosia in which they argued that the patient's recognition problems were due to a disruption in the processes that combine parts of objects into perceptual wholes. As we show (see Chapter 4), this account was, to some extent, a precursor of our own.

Bay re-examined Goldstein and Gelb's patient some 20 years later and was annoyed at what he felt were inconsistencies in the patient's performance. Furthermore, the patient behaved in an awkward, stereotyped manner in the test situation which was quite different from his manner in the social situation. Bay argued that the patient had probably suffered from some form of intellectual damage in addition to the damage which resulted in problems of visual recognition. Bay later contended that most cases of visual agnosia had a history of cerebro-vascular disease rather than the more localised disorders caused by brain tumour or head injury. Cerebro-vascular disease may affect large areas of the brain and could conceivably affect intellectual functioning.

Writers subsequent to Bay have strongly denied that the label of "dementia" could apply to their visual agnosic patients. For example, Pallis (1955) described his patient to be "of above average intelligence and his general awareness was very keen". Bornstein and Kidron (1959) state of their patient that "no intellectual deterioration was noted at any time nor was any change seen in the critical faculties or memory". Of his patient Kertesz (1979) writes: "Behaviourally she did not resemble dementia at all, she was very quick to use non-visual cues for recognition". Indeed, Bay himself was able to study a case of visual agnosia in an intelligent man who showed no evidence of dementia (Bay, 1953). This discovery led Bay to moderate his views and he no longer claimed that part of the syndrome of visual agnosia was necessarily intellectual deterioration.

Nonetheless, it is clear that dementia is a convenient label to apply when aspects of behaviour are not fully understood. For example, why is it that an agnosic patient can recognise some objects but not others? Ettlinger and Wyke put this problem to a formal test (1961). They argued that it may be easier for an agnosic patient to identify more-familiar than less-familiar items. They asked their patient to name a number of items and these were divided into groups comprising: 1) Familiar objects; 2) Less familiar objects; and 3) Unfamiliar objects. They found no relationship in their patient between failure of identification and the degree of familiarity of the objects. If anything, there were fewer (rather than more) errors with the unfamiliar objects than with the familiar ones. Thus, there appeared to be no apparent explanation for the paradoxical behaviour of the agnosic patient, and "dementia" was an easy label to apply.

A SUMMARY

From our brief discussion, it is apparent that brain damage can affect human behaviour in many different ways. Some effects are very specific, influencing some behaviours but not others. The term "visual agnosia" refers to one such selective deficit, concerning the visual recognition of common objects. This is a rare disorder, and so has been viewed with scepticism on occasions. Given this scepticism, studies of agnosic patients must query whether the initial processing of visual information is intact in the patient, and whether there are intellectual deficits that might impinge on the object recognition process. If we are to draw any insights about normal visual recognition from such cases, we must ensure that any disorders are specific to the recognition process.

We need also to consider the precise nature of the problems encountered by individual patients so that we can make parallels between the patient's problem and particular aspects of the normal recognition process. With these points in mind then, we may turn to consider John's case.

2 The History of a Case of Visual Agnosia

CASE HISTORY

Until April 1981, the course of John's life was not dissimilar from the courses of many other lives. It had had its high spots and low spots, its moments of personal happiness and success, its moments of failure. John was educated at a boarding school in England, while his parents were abroad in India. He trained to be an aeroplane pilot and spent the initial part of the Second World War stationed in France with the R.A.F. Later he transferred to become a member of a tank regiment. During the war he married Iris. Following the war he worked in a firm engaged in the manufacture of metal windows for houses. He was later employed by an American company which was concerned with the control of solar heat and ultra violet radiation. He rose to an executive position, and had responsibility for marketing within Europe.

In 1981 John's life changed dramatically. He was taken ill and had an emergency operation for a perforated appendix. Post-operatively, he suffered a stroke. John had had a history of artrial fibrillation (uneven contractions of the upper chambers of the heart). It is possible that this heart condition could have resulted in a small blood clot travelling to the brain, blocking one of the smaller arteries supplying the brain and causing the death of brain tissue. The resulting condition is commonly termed a "stroke".

At first it was not obvious to those concerned that he had had a stroke. As we discussed in Chapter 1 (p. 19) strokes occur commonly as a result of damage to the middle cerebral artery of the brain. Patients with damage here often develop a paralysis on one side of the body (termed a hemiplegia). In John's case, the damage was in the region of the posterior cerebral artery, affecting the occipital lobes at the back of the brain. Since this area of the brain is quite removed from those areas controlling movement, damage does not produce associated paralysis. Doctors and nurses caring for patients following surgery are well aware that there is a very slight risk of the patient having a stroke, and watch carefully for any sign of weakness on one side of the body. No weakness was apparent in John's case, but he did seem to behave in a very strange way. He didn't seem able to recognise the doctors and nurses who attended him, he would get lost when trying to find his way to the bathroom, despite having been shown the way on numerous occasions, and he complained that he was unable to read. There is always some degree of stress associated with surgery, and it is not unknown for patients subsequently to show a degree of confusion and disorientation. These symptoms, however, do not persist, and medical staff are trained to provide re-assurance for as long as the symptoms last. This is what happened in John's case, but, surprisingly, his confusion did not abate. John's recollection of the early days is quite clear. He writes:

My first memory is of being aware of that dreadful unending clatter of clashing metal containers, cutlery, and serving trollies ringing in, apparently, hypersensitive ears, mingling with that sickening, all-pervading smell of cheap, "general" disinfectant which told my slowly awakening brain that I was in a hospital. Of that, I was categorically certain; the sounds and smells were instantly acceptable. I don't suppose the events of the next few minutes was much different to the normal return to full consciousness after any anaesthesia. The most puzzling next event was my wife's first visit. I recognised her voice quite easily, but put down to some sort of hangover any certainty of seeing her properly. On her leaving, I remember quite clearly assuring myself that some temporary "bang on the head" was affecting my vision. Because I was in hospital, I was presented at breakfast time with a menu showing what was on offer for the next two days, and I was asked to mark my ticket for the next half-dozen meals. Because I was kept very well changed and shaven etc. by my visiting wife, it was assumed by the nurses that I must be a difficult patient because I kept handing back the menu cards uncompleted. It was my wife who discovered I had completely lost the ability to read. Thank goodness, though, she had the sense and determination to return the very next day with a pack of "lexicon" cards. She literally started by having me read single letters and then two- or three-letter words.

When something totally inexplicable befalls one, the overriding initial response is to hope that it will go away. In the meantime, one tries to manage everyday activities in as normal a fashion as possible. It seems reasonable to suggest, therefore, that because John was trying to cope with each new problem as it arose, he was unable to appreciate the real magnitude of his problem as a whole. The same is not true of his wife who, as a close outside observer, quickly became painfully aware of the totality of the problem. Her dismay is clearly expressed:

A day or two after my husband's operation I knew something was seriously wrong. The medical and nursing staff assured me that he was just suffering post-operative shock, but this did not allay my fears. Each day when I visited him there was additional evidence of his problems. The fact that he would ask visitors, at short intervals, what the time or day was and could not remember what he had eaten for lunch a few minutes previously was strange, but I thought this could be post-operative shock. However, the day I arrived with flowers and he asked me what they were really worried me, and caused me to ask what colour they and the curtains of the ward were. Grey was the reply, and a few further questions ascertained that suddenly he was completely colour blind.

That night I went home distressed knowing that I had to face the fact that, whatever the doctors said, something had affected his brain and life for him would never be the same again. I knew he had not been able to see the sketches or read the words on his get-well cards and I spent the night thinking of ways in which I could help him. Next day I took in some lexicon cards and when I asked him the names of the letters he got several wrong. Each day I continued this game and gradually he could read words of three letters. He would spell them out by letter: "m", "a", "p", "map"—though sometimes this would become "mad" not "map". Longer words at this stage defeated him.

Encouraged by the fact that he could remember events months or years before, I gave him a piece of paper and asked him to sign his name. Imagine my joy and relief when he produced a perfect signature quickly and with all the usual dots and loops! I followed this up by suggesting that he wrote a few lines to thank someone for their good wishes. This was not a good effort, some words were repeated and some letters such as "p" and "d" or "s" and "z" were mixed up. He was also unable to read back what he had written, so, after an interruption for a cup of tea, I had to read back the last sentence. Unfortunately an hour afterwards he had forgotten he had written it and asked me to write to his friend.

He had been moved to a small ward with only six or eight beds, but was upset because he could not find his way to the cloakroom. At Easter other patients in the ward were allowed home for the holiday so for two hours we were able to walk backwards and forwards to the cloakroom to try and learn the route. In the end he was able to manage the trip by himself, so next day I asked his ward mate whether he had gone there by himself.

"No, he had to be brought back from the corridor", was the disappointing reply.

The neurologists were troubled by his lack of progress and thought a return to his home surroundings would be helpful, so, four weeks after the operation, arrangements were made for his wound to be dressed at home and he was discharged.

Being unsure of his reactions to a car journey, I asked a friend to drive us in his car and kept John talking to keep his mind off the traffic.

"Why do we stop here?" he asked when the car stopped.

"You live here." I replied.

"Really?" he answered.

We walked into the house and he looked around as though he had never been there before. After some days he could find his way from room to room but could not recognise ornaments, pictures or furniture. It seemed important to him to feel he could do some things unaided so for several days I took him to the post-box, about 50 yards down the road on the same side of the street. One day I suggested that he could save me time by going to the post on his own. Watching from the window I saw him walk quite confidently in the right direction and all went well until, on the return trip, he walked past the house. Luckily we lived at the end of a cul-de-sac so he realised his error and turned back but stood for many minutes at the top of our steps before deciding that it was our house.

John's return home, for him, led to a realisation and a gradual coming to terms with his deficit. He writes:

I have to say that my first few days back at home caused such a disappointment with the firmly expressed medical opinion that "all would click back quite simply", that in some ways confidence in anyone became more restricted. This period lasted some time, during which I fell into tantrums caused by very minor problems following my inability to carry out simple everyday tasks, and most particularly if I read criticism into a comment or action. One of our remaining pleasures at the time was minding the dogs of a friend. Whilst doing this one weekend I read criticism into some very innocent comment from my wife and just swept the whole kitchen table load of china to the floor, and flounced off into the garden like some hysterical girl—behaviour unlikely and most certainly disapproved by my grandfather status. During my first few months at home various such flare-ups occurred; they were short-lasting. On one occasion I lost my temper whilst helping my wife in the garden. Again I read "complaint" into something she said. By mischance I had a long-handled garden fork in my hands, and promptly threw it—well, perhaps if not directly at her, then very near her, where it stuck into the ground. I stormed off out of the garden, onto the nearby common hillside, and stamped across to the woodlands edging it. I reached there perhaps in a few minutes, breathless, and was then rapidly "cooled-off" by the realisation that I had no idea how to go home again; it was no good looking back; I knew there was a gate into the grassed area from the road where the house stood, but I could not recognise it. My hot temper cooled very rapidly as I had to work out from memory that as long as I travelled down-hill and followed the line of the trees and undergrowth which bordered three sides of the grassy hillside, I could reach the wicket-gate into our road. Fortunately though, I didn't have to make the journey alone as my better half had already set off to rescue me! I instance these as a couple of the more ludicrous actions I took during the initial few months after returning home.

John had been discharged home in the hope that familiar surroundings might decrease his post-operative "confusion". His symptoms continued, though; he was unable to recognise familiar faces, the familiar objects around his home, he got lost when he ventured outside, he could only read slowly and with great effort, and, though he could write he could not read back what he had written; he had also lost the ability to perceive colour. The world had become black, white, and shades of grey.

It was becoming increasingly apparent that John had suffered some form of brain damage. A computed tomography (CT) scan was ordered; this is currently the procedure of choice in the diagnosis of the vast array of known or suspected abnormalities of the brain. Relative to some procedures, it is quite painless. The technique is based on the computer analysis of the absorption of X-ray photons which are passed through the skull and brain from various angles. A cross-sectional image is then reconstructed by computer. It allows brain lesions to be identified with a high degree of accuracy. In John's case, however, the initial CT scan showed no evidence of damage to the brain.

Iris found it hard to believe that there was no brain damage in view of John's strikingly abnormal behaviour. She wrote, therefore, to his doctor:

... I find it hard to accept that his visual difficulties could be accounted for by a nervous breakdown, but then my knowledge of such things is nil! He is still totally colour blind and also seems to have no visual pictures in his memory. For example, he cannot tell the difference between different leaf shapes or differentiate between flowers and leaves in the garden, which prevents him enjoying his favourite hobby of gardening. He can still not recognise even me by sight and, if waiting for me outside a shop, will look blankly or perhaps, uncertainly, at me until I begin to speak.

He does not see pictures and cannot describe the subject matter of those we have had in the house for years.

His reading is restricted to newspaper headlines or large print books which he can read only for short periods before his eyes start watering. The speed of reading is very slow. As reading was his favourite relaxation, he finds this disability very frustrating.

His letter writing has improved. The first attempts contained a number of repeated words but this now seldom happens. He does, however, sometimes write wrong letters, the most frequent being "p" for "d" or "z" for "s" and he often mixes up "p" and "d" when he reads aloud to me.

His factual long term memory seems reasonable and he can converse well. We do the Daily Telegraph crossword puzzles with me reading the clues; he contributes quite a good number of answers remembering books, quotations, and odd words. He can also recall the names of men and the facts about jobs connected with his past business. Contrary to this, he cannot find his way around our local town or recognise any roads when we drive around the local area which he has known for over twenty years. After about four trips I now let him go to the post box thirty yards away on the same side of the street as at last he has learnt to recognise our house. Sometimes in the town he thinks he knows where he is, but unfortunately, he is never right.

The short-term memory is still giving him problems but more so when associated with sight. He is continually putting things in the wrong place even if I tell him where they go a minute before. If I ask him to fetch a glass or cup he opens nearly every cupboard in the kitchen before finding the right one. To solve the problem of him not remembering how to turn the T.V. and radio on I have had to put white adhesive tape on the "on" button. He can see the T.V. but he describes it as a poor black and white picture and he does not recognise the faces . . . .

The doctor referred John to the clinical psychologist for an assessment. It was important to establish whether his strange behaviour had an organic (physical) or non-organic (mental) basis. A clinical psychologist will use a number of standardised tests in the course of an assessment, and measures will be taken of the patient's intelligence, sensory-motor ability and so forth. The patient's scores are then compared to the scores of subjects from a similar age bracket, but who have not suffered brain damage. The assessment of John showed that he was selectively bad at many of the visual tests, but quite unimpaired at tests requiring verbal knowledge. This picture of a selective visual problem is consistent with physical damage to those areas of the brain concerned with vision.

The CT scan had not shown such damage. However, sometimes, when the scan is carried out quite close to the time when the stroke occurred abnormalities are not detected. This is because it takes some time before the dead tissue assumes a characteristic appearance. A further CT scan, some three years later, in fact showed extensive brain damage in both occipital lobes in the areas supplied by the posterior cerebral artery (see Fig. 2.1).

Subsequently, more detailed tests of John's vision were conducted. He was shown to have normal acuity using the standard Snellan charts. Also, the full extent of his vision in different parts of his visual field was assessed,

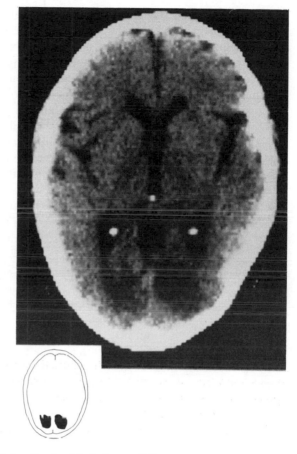

FIG. 2.1. CT scan performed on John, showing a bilateral lesion in the region supplied by the posterior cerebral artery. The marked areas on the inset diagram indicate the lesions.

by asking him to detect lights flashed briefly to different areas of the field and at different brightnesses. The results indicated that he had lost his vision in the top two halves of both his left and his right visual fields. As we discussed earlier in Chapter 1, this field defect is characteristic of patients with cerebral achromatopsia (i.e., the complete loss of colour vision following brain damage), and it can be taken as indicating a lesion to the prestriate cortex in the region of the lower pathway leading to the temporal lobe. Because of this field defect, we might expect that when John looks at someone's eyes he would not see the top of their head, or that when he looks at the door of a house he would not see the roof. However, John automatically makes slight movements of his head and eyes to allow him to see everything with the intact portions of his visual field. It does not seem that this field defect in itself should cause the massive recognition problem he suffers; indeed, after brain damage patients may quite often have some form of field defect, which may prevent them noticing objects that appear in the "blind" field, but it is only rarely that a patient has agnosia so that he or she cannot recognise an object once it has been noticed.

Establishing that some sort of damage exists is, however, far from the end of the story. We need to know exactly what processes in vision have become difficult for John. The problem in doing this is illustrated by an example of his behaviour noted by one of the doctors: "Whilst weeding, he will disturb his wife by pulling out the annual planting, yet he will cut a hedge without any difficulty—but then he will continue with the shears straight into the roses." In some senses, John can "see", since he is able to cut the hedge, yet in others he cannot, since he fails to discriminate plants from weeds, or the hedge from rose bushes. Perhaps if we can begin to understand the "whys" in this sort of case we can begin to understand how visual processes operate in the undamaged brain.

We were interested to discover the "why" of the visual breakdown, and count ourselves fortunate, in many ways, to be introduced to John. It was made clear to him that, because so little was known about the processes impaired in visual agnosia, or about how such processes might be rehabilitated, we could not guarantee to help him in any way. He would to all intents and purposes be our "guinea-pig". He was quite content with this and signed himself so on odd occasions!

We first saw John about two months after his stroke. By that time, many of the initial problems that are often associated with brain damage, such as patients repeating themselves or rapidly forgetting what has been said to them, had receded. We found him an articulate and insightful man, very willing to undertake our many tedious tasks.

How does one begin to study "why" a patient such as John has such massive visual recognition problems? One is presented with a conundrum, a jigsaw puzzle comprising a great number of pieces. These pieces are made up of the tasks the patient is able to do, as well as the tasks he or she is unable to do. One's initial hunch about where the pieces should go represents one's starting conceptions about agnosia. Clearly, one needs to be careful not to force the pieces together simply on the basis of this hunch.

The beginning of research in such cases must be to set some parameters within which one can begin to work. These are perhaps akin to the edges of the jigsaw. In order to set the parameters one must have a clear description of the problem and this is provided in an extremely detailed and insightful way by John. The following paragraphs illustrate some of the questions one might wish to ask, together with John's answers collected over our years of testing him.

Are you able to describe your visual problem to us?

To try and explain how I now see the world is quite difficult; somehow what I'm seeing can't be easily captured in words. If I try hard the nearest description I can get to is to say that everything is slightly out of focus, though not to my eyes if you understand, but to my brain. However, this is really inadequate. I know from an optical point of view that my lens-corrected vision is as good as can be achieved—and my vision has been extensively examined to ensure that there were no obvious reasons which might inhibit my recognition of things. I therefore harbour no irrational ideas that there will be any sudden cure, such as the design of some new glasses.

How do you manage with the recognition of common objects?

I have come to cope with recognising many common objects, if they are standing alone, and I manage in the flat by trying to keep things in the same place—just as if I were blind. When objects are placed together, though, I have more difficulties. For instance, eating at a buffet or self-service restaurant is extremely difficult, especially bearing in mind that I only see in black and white. At one time, at a buffet, I mistook horse-radish sauce for cream and poured it on my strawberries—only to be unpleasantly surprised. Also, although I can recognise many food items seen individually, they somehow seem hard to separate *en masse*. To recognise one sausage on its own is far from picking one out from a dish of cold foods in a salad: a case of "can't see the trees for the wood"?

Generally, I find moving objects much easier to recognise, presumably because I see different and changing views—it is a normal human reaction, after all, to give oneself several different and moving views of an unknown object when seeking to recognise it. For that reason the T.V. screen enables me to comprehend far more of an outdoor scene than, for example, the drawings on my living room walls which I have known for a lifetime, but now cannot recognise.

For many years an excellent etching of St. Paul's Cathedral in London, drawn by an outstanding contemporary A.R.A., of the bomb-cleared era of London during the '39–'45 war, has hung on our living-room wall. I know the building has the famous dome-shaped roof and I can point it out in detail on the picture. But now it does not "fit" my memory of the picture nor of the reality. Knowing that I should be able to identify the general design of the dome-headed, high circular central tower covering a particularly cruciform building, I can point out the expected detail but cannot recognise the whole structure. On the other hand I am sure I could draw a reasonable copy of the picture. The reason I say this is that I can see very clearly every detail of objects even if I do not always recognise the whole. Pictures are much more difficult if the artist has used shade, reflection or the skills of impressionism (rather than directly portraying trees, water or a cloudscape, say).

Mostly, I am able to recognise the general class that an object belongs to—such as whether it is an animal or a bird; but I cannot tell which particular bird or animal it is. This problem is not confined to animate objects. For instance, we recently went to the R.A.F. museum at Hendon. I knew well in advance I was to see an old Lysander which I used to fly in '39 to '40 (until I went into the army). Now, a Lysander is very different in general shape from most aircraft ever made and distinguishable to a degree. The odd thing was, that when we came to the display I did not see it in "toto". I recalled enough to tell the others to pick out details and where to find them and had them laughing when I remembered the ludicrous instructions for the rear gunner to bale out in a hurry etc. and even where certain equipment not on display used to be fitted. But in all honesty, I did not recognise the "whole".

Although you are not able to recognise objects when you see them, are you able to remember what a particular object should look like?

To draw from memory I don't find too difficult, bearing in mind that I never had much drawing ability or the simplest comprehension of how to show a third dimension in scribblings. On the other hand, my mind knows very clearly what I should like to draw and I can comprehend enough of my own handiwork to know if it is a reasonable representation of what I had in mind. However, there are a few objects which I can no longer recall to mind— particularly some flowers, for which I remember the botanical names but no longer their appearance.

What about recognising faces?

Probably my most embarrassing problem is not recognising people. Since coming round I have never been able to recognise any person by sight alone. I cannot recognise my wife except by sound of her voice, nor my grandchildren, nor family nor friends. I also have great problems with animals, particularly if they are not moving.

Friends and business acquaintances of long standing, like the milkman and the G.P., I recognise by sound. Of my generation, most of the men wear trousers of instep length and sport haircuts shorter than their wives and daughters. I frequently free the inner side of the pavements to long-haired, short-trousered teenaged boys who probably have no conception of convention anyway!

I have learned that to recognise people its often easiest to use non-facial clues—an obvious example is hair length and general pattern. My colour problem can also cause extra difficulties as I don't differentiate between blondes and grey-haired ladies. I recall mannerisms shown by friends and family—the use of arms when speaking, ear scratching, ways of standing, all visual aids to identify them in parties and groups where the auditory clues are too confused or numerous for separation.

Awaiting my wife's exit from supermarkets, I have astonished strange ladies by picking up their shopping and walking away with it, under the impression that it was my wife I had been watching pass through the pay desk! On occasions travelling to town, she or my grandchildren ask me to identify animals in the fields; if the animals are static, I'm often wrong. The same goes for buildings. Even with major London buildings I'm often at a loss except for very obvious and clear standing examples like the Albert Hall, which I can get from its dome.

Are you able to recognise yourself in a mirror?

Well, I can certainly see a face, with eyes, nose and mouth etc., but somehow it's not familiar; it really could be anybody. I can also see enough to decide whether my now-limited hair is tidy or in need of a brush, but at the same time as this I don't seem to have enough detail to know whether I need a shave or whether my face is dirty. But I can see the tiny scarred notch on my nose and recall how and where it was caused, years ago.

What about colour vision?

I only see objects in shades of grey. This lack of colour vision is quite annoying in relationship to everyday living. I am unsure of matching pairs of socks of similar length and fabric, and certainly I am bad at choosing the appropriate tie for a shirt or jacket.

Are you able to read?

Of all my problems, I find that of being reduced to reading so slowly, the most frustrating on an everyday basis. The problem simplified is that the mental exercise involved in making sense of the letters in order to create a word requires so much mental effort that I often have forgotten the overall content of a sentence, requiring re-reading in order to comprehend the whole. I also find great difficulty in reading my own longhand, let alone that of others.

How do you manage to find your way about?

This is another major problem. An extension of my initial problem of not knowing the geography of my house is the still-continuing difficulty of not recognising my surroundings and consequently of not knowing my where-abouts. A small collection of local shops is about 240 paces away from the entrance of the flat we have since moved to. I know this because it took my patient wife more than 12 months teaching before I could do it "solo". The local post office is about 10 minutes walk away; I am now convinced, after three years since moving here, that I could find my way there, but my instructor will not yet trust me! Along with this there is a subsidiary difficulty. I am not good at judging distances or the speed of road traffic, so we tend to be cautious in sending me out for errands! Also because of this problem with distances and speeds, I am an incredibly bad front-seat passenger. The generality of my discomfort in this situation arises from my own conviction that the car is much nearer to the vehicle in front than is really true.

When I do go to the shops I can manage perfectly well until I meet friends *en route* and stop to chat. I can then be quite disorientated, and have to re-orient myself either by asking them or by walking on until I recognise a salient point from which to continue the journey. Quite recently, due to "not thinking what I was doing", I had to return to my last recognised check-point, our block of flats, to recommence the short journey to the shops.

It has crossed family minds as to what I should do were I to get badly lost. In a town, during normal hours, I would just ask a passer-by, take a taxi home or, if really desparate, find my way by asking a policeman! I have not yet had to do this, but I hope I could explain my predicament to the puzzled public! Fortunately, I have not lost my social skills and, could I find a hotel in a strange town, am quite capable of organising an overnight room and meals until I could be rescued! I have also not become fearful in public places but rather hypercritical of the ill manners—imagined or otherwise—of people. I suppose I have turned out to be rather crustier than I should, but that has always been the privilege of seniority!

SOME GENERAL CONCLUSIONS

From John's description of his problems, it is clear that he is suffering visual agnosia. However, the classification of John as an agnosic patient is but the start of our attempt to understand why he finds visual recognition so difficult. We need to know the kind of agnosia involved and, most especially, which processes in visual recognition he finds difficult. To further our understanding, we must consider the processes normally mediating visual recognition. Chapter 3 provides an overview of these processes. In Chapter 4 we return to John's case, and we present an analysis of his problem in terms of the account of visual recognition developed in Chapter 3.

3

The Process of Visual Object Recognition

Perhaps the most common view outside the world of the visual perception laboratory is that vision corresponds to a picture projected from the eye to the brain. A fuller outline of this view has recently been discussed (though not advocated) by Professor John Frisby of Sheffield University. He writes (Frisby, 1979; p. 8):

Each eye works like a camera. Both camera and eye have a lens, and where the camera has light-sensitive film, the eye has a light-sensitive retina, a network of tiny receptive units that form the back surface of the eyeball. The lens's job is to focus an image of the outside world on to the retina—the retinal image—which stimulates the retina so that it sends messages about the image along optic nerve fibres to the brain. The brain is composed of millions of tiny components called cells. Certain cells specialise in vision and are arranged in the form of a sheet—the "inner screen". Each cell in the screen can at any moment be either active or inactive. If a cell is very active, it is signalling the presence of a bright spot at that particular point of the "inner screen"—and hence at the associated point in the outside world. Equally, if a cell is only moderately active, it is signalling an intermediate shade of grey. Completely inactive cells signal black spots. Cells in the "inner screen" as a whole take on a pattern of activity whose overall shape directly mirrors the shape of the retinal image received by the eye. For example, if a painting is being observed as in [Fig. 3.1], then the pattern of activity on the "inner screen" directly resembles the painting. As soon as this pattern is set up on the screen of cells, the observer has the experience of seeing the painting.

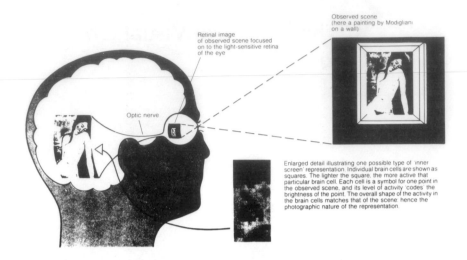

Fig. 3.1. The "inner screen" theory of vision (from Frisby, 1979). Painting reproduced by permission of the Courtauld Institute Galleries, London (Courtauld Collection).

This theory, then, proposes that there is an exact one-to-one correspondence between points in the image of the outside world and both the relative locations and levels of activity of cells in the brain. Neighbouring cells are thought to respond to neighbouring points in the image, with the degree of activity in the cells representing the brightness of the image points. However, in Chapter 1 we discussed evidence showing that many brain areas are involved in the visual recognition of a given object, with

FIG. 3.2. (a) The Müller-Lyer illusion (from Gregory, 1970). Specific accounts of the illusion differ. One proposal is that it is due to processes which, unbeknown to the observer, code the relative depths of points in the figure and which scale the points according to the depth information. The fins pointing out suggest that the central line is farther away than it would appear in isolation, and the fins pointing in suggest that the line is closer. Now, objects which have the same size but which are at different depths project different-sized images on the retina—with the further object projecting a smaller image. The idea is that this size-depth relationship is taken into account when judging the size of the central line. Because the line surrounded by the outwards-pointing fins is taken as farther away, and because its retinal image is the same size as that of the other central line, it must (in reality) be longer. What we become conscious of is this interpretation of what must be the real lengths of the lines, consequently we "see" the illusion (e.g., Gregory, 1970).

However, this is by no means the only possible explanation. It could be that the effect has nothing to do with the explicit coding of depth. For instance, suppose that, when asked to judge the length of the central line, we cannot help "pooling" information from its surrounding context. Because the outwards-pointing fins extend away from the central line, they tend to increase judgements of its length (see Robinson, 1972).

(b) A real-world example of the Müller-Lyer illusion.

a

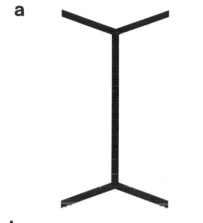

b

each of these areas performing a different function. The activity in the brain during the recognition of an object does not in any simple way resemble an inner screen. This point is also brought home by the psychological studies of the processes involved in object recognition to which we now turn.

ILLUSIONS AND THE INNER SCREEN

Visual illusions provide some of the most striking examples to illustrate that visual recognition involves processing and coding of input, and not just the registration of that input on an inner screen. Consider Fig. 3.2, which depicts perhaps the most famous of all illusions, the Müller-Lyer. The

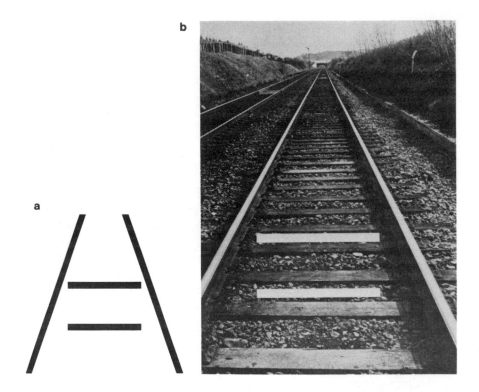

FIG. 3.3.   (a) The Ponzo illusion; (b) a real-world example of the Ponzo illusion (from Gregory, 1970).

Müller-Lyer illusion is composed of two vertical lines, each having two fins at each end. In one instance the fins point away from the line, in the other they point towards it. The vertical lines are in fact the same length, though the line with the fins pointing away from it appears longer. Similarly, consider the Ponzo illusion, shown in Fig. 3.3. The two horizontal lines in this figure are also the same length, though we tend to judge the upper horizontal line as longer than the lower one. Such illusions are not the sole preserve of the laboratory, and similar effects can quite easily be demonstrated in real-world settings (see Figs. 3.2b and 3.3b). Our point in presenting these illusions is to illustrate that vision does not involve the faithful reproduction of external stimuli; if that were true we would never be "tricked" into seeing lines as differing in length when they are, in fact, the same. These illusions show that our perception of visual stimuli, even of single lines, is influenced by the surrounding context. The visual system does not code lines as discrete entities, rather it codes and uses information about the relations between lines. This coding of the relations between lines could not take place if vision simply involved the registration of stimuli on an inner screen.

THE GESTALT APPROACH

Unfortunately, though illusions serve as eye-catching demonstration tools, and though they are clearly contrary to an inner screen notion, the processes involved in generating the effects remain imperfectly understood (see the Fig. 3.2 caption). This means that the illusions themselves are imperfect tools for investigating the processes mediating visual recognition. What is needed is research concerned with these processes.

Some of the earliest work that treated visual recognition as a process was conducted by psychologists belonging to what has come to be known as the Gestalt school. The Gestalt school of psychology began in Germany in the early years of the twentieth century, and was characterised by the use of introspection to document the process of form perception, and by the view that "the whole is greater than the sum of its parts". That is, that our perception of complex forms often cannot be characterised in terms of the independent coding of the parts making up the forms. Instead, perception is based on information specific to the configuration of the parts (a Gestalt).

The Müller-Lyer and Ponzo illusions (Figs. 3.2 and 3.3) both show that we do not treat form elements independently of the visual context in which they appear. The Gestalt psychologists went beyond this in that they tried to formulate a set of rules governing the coding of individual form elements, which had implications for how a given form would be seen as a

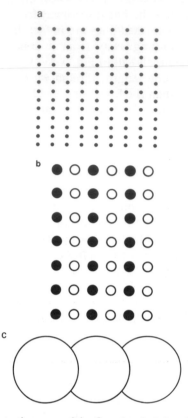

FIG. 3.4. Examples illustrating some of the Gestalt principles of perceptual organization. a) The principle of proximity—the dots are seen as forming vertical columns because their vertical spacing is narrower than their horizontal spacing. b) The principle of similarity—the dots group on the basis of having similar colours. c) The principle of closure—the circles are seen as complete (i.e. closed) figures which are overlapping each other, rather than as incomplete (open) figures lying flat in-the-plane (in two-dimensions).

whole. For instance, they argued that elements which are close together in time and/or space will tend to be seen as belonging together (they will tend to "group"; this is termed the "principle of proximity"), that elements which look similar will be grouped together (the "principle of similarity"), that elements which move together will be grouped together (the "principle of common fate"), and that elements will tend to group to form a "closed" rather than an "open" figure (the "principle of closure") (see Fig. 3.4 for examples).

These principles are concerned with the ways in which form information is organised during visual perception. For instance, the principles state that lines which are close together and at the same orientation will be coded together, and tend to appear as part of the same object. There is also another feature of perceptual organisation, identified by the Gestalt psychologists, which actually underpins each of the examples shown in Fig. 3.4. In each of these examples, the visual system is presented with information which could be organised in various different ways (for instance, the dots in Fig. 3.4a could be seen as forming horizontal rows rather than vertical columns). The principles formulated by the Gestalt psychologists concerned the factors determining the organisation we initially perceive; but, in forming these perceptions, what we are actually doing is coding one organisation as the "figure" present whilst the other information in the stimulus is coded as the "background". Perceptual organisation is built on our ability to segment the world into what is "figure" and what is "ground". In the examples shown in Fig. 3.4, where the stimulus information is consistent with only one of the Gestalt principles, it is quite difficult to realise that other organisations are possible. This is shown more dramatically by pictures that take on different identities according to which part is coded as the figure and which as the ground, a famous example being the ambiguous vase-face picture, shown in Fig. 3.5. Again, examples of the importance of figure-ground separation are not confined to the laboratory. In the real world, camouflage serves precisely to make difficult the separation of a figure from its background (see Fig. 3.6).

FIG. 3.5.   The ambiguous vase-face figure (from Rubin, 1915).

FIG. 3.6.   An example of camouflage. Photograph by P. Ward. Copyright © Bruce Coleman Ltd. Used by permission.

The Gestalt approach thus emphasised that visual recognition is based on particular organisations imposed upon the world and that the principles of perceptual organisation are themselves based on general characteristics of stimuli (such as the proximity and visual similarity of form elements), and not on characteristics specific to the objects involved. We return to this point when we consider John's case in more detail.

LIMITATIONS OF THE GESTALT APPROACH AND SOME REMAINING ISSUES

Major limitations to the Gestalt approach were caused by the Gestalt psychologists bringing with them certain ideas about how their principles of perceptual organisation were implemented in the brain. One of these ideas was that every visual experience was partnered by a brain event that paralled the nature of the experience. That is, there was thought to be a trace in the brain which was isomorphic with the object which was perceived, so that the trace was square if the object was square, and it was round if the object was round, etc. These traces were thought to be controlled by "field forces", akin to magnetic fields, which constrained the traces to be as stable as possible (with a "closed" figure being more stable than an open one, for instance). This view has characteristics in common with the inner screen theory (Fig. 3.1), in that there is thought to be a one-to-one relationship between the properties of the object and the brain events underlying its perception. However, because many brain areas are involved in visual perception (Chapter 1), we may conclude that any theory suggesting that recognition is based on one-to-one correspondences between external and brain events is mistaken.

There are also limitations to the Gestalt approach to the coding principles upon which perceptual organisation is based. One such limitation concerns the failure to provide a detailed exposition of the relations between the parts of an object and the object considered as a whole. For instance, take the "fruit-face" stimulus shown in Fig. 3.7. Each "part" of this stimulus can be interpreted as a piece of fruit; the "whole" stimulus, on the other hand, is best interpreted as a face. In this example, the identity assigned to the "whole" figure is quite different to that assigned to each of its parts. It is as if the process of assigning identity to the whole figure operates independently of those involved in assigning identities to each of its parts. Indeed, we could replace the pieces of fruit with almost any object and, providing the spatial relations between the "parts" remain approximately the same, we would still identify the "whole" as a face. On the other hand, details concerning the particular visual characteristics of the parts, and of their local relations, are important when we are asked to recognise an object as a specific member of its class. The identification of a

FIG. 3.7.   The fruit-face figure (from Palmer, 1975a).

particular face, for instance, depends crucially on details such as the size of the eyes, and of their local relations relative to each other and to the nose. If we are to identify the owner of the face, we cannot substitute the "parts" of the face willy nilly. It is therefore possible to distinguish between what we might call a "first pass" coding of an object, which uses only general information about local parts, and a more detailed coding of the parts and their relations. First pass coding is often sufficient for us to identify the general class of an object (e.g., that it is a face), but not its specific identity (e.g., whose face it is). The Gestalt approach gives us some indication of how local forms combine to generate perceptual wholes, but it fails to distinguish different types of coding (such as first pass and detailed codings) and the purposes to which they may be put. Some of the questions we might ask here are whether first pass coding does occur, and, whether this first pass operates independently of the processes involved in coding in detail the visual characteristics of the local elements.

In other circumstances, however, our judgements of the identity of the "parts" of objects can be shown to depend on their being perceived as part of a whole. Consider Fig. 3.8. The facial features in this figure are difficult to identify when seen in isolation, and they may only be clearly identified when assigned their correct positions within the "whole" face. We need to ask here, what are the circumstances determining when information about the "whole" guides identification of the parts—is it only when "part" information is ambiguous, or can it occur with unambiguous "part" information? Also, how does "whole" information affect "part" identification—does it affect our representation of the parts (e.g., do we *see* the parts as more eye-, nose- or mouth-like when they are in the face?), or does it only act to bias our responses? These questions, though important

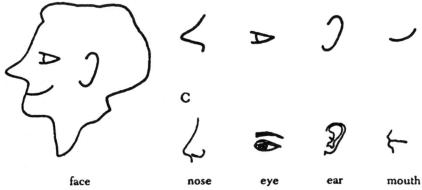

| face | nose | eye | ear | mouth |

FIG. 3.8.   A face with ambiguous parts (from Palmer, 1975a).

FIG. 3.9.   An etching by Hogarth (from Gregory, 1970).

for generating a detailed theory of visual recognition, were not addressed by the Gestalt psychologists.

In discussing the relations between perceptual wholes and their parts, we have only considered single objects. However, in the real world we are faced with "whole" scenes in which the "parts" are single objects. The Gestalt approach did not stretch to a consideration of scene recognition, or how scene recognition might relate to the processes involved in the recognition of single objects. Nevertheless, the two tasks appear to have at least some common processes. Figure 3.9 shows an engraving of a fisherman, produced by William Hogarth in 1754. At first glance, the scene portrayed appears to be perfectly normal. Closer inspection, however, reveals incongruities between where various objects lie in depth (e.g., note the fisherman's rod, the sign on the inn and so forth). Hogarth has toyed with perspective to produce a picture which could not be realised in the world. The picture still maintains a semblance of normality, though, because the local relations between the objects at each point in the scene are correct. For instance, the trees occlude the sign of the inn, giving a local cue to indicate that the sign is behind the trees; it is only when one also notes that the sign is attached to the inn and that there are other clues, both of size and occlusion, indicating that the inn is some way in front of the trees, that the incongruities are apparent. There is thus a paradox between the local cues to the relations between the objects in depth, and the incongruous depth relations across wider (more global) areas of the picture. That we find it difficult to perceive these incongruities at a glance suggests that we build information about scenes on the basis of the relations between local parts of the scene, and that more global relations between objects are only coded subsequently.

Consider now the "impossible triangle" devised by L. S. and R. Penrose (Fig. 3.10). Like the Hogarth engraving, the impossible triangle contains local cues about the angles of the joints which are inconsistent with one another. However, we again find it difficult to pick up the impossibility of the figure at a glance. Thus both scene and object recognition seem to

FIG. 3.10.   The ambiguous triangle (from Gregory, 1970).

require processes that integrate local codings of the relations between parts of the object or scene, to form a globally consistent interpretation. Unfortunately, we know little about the relation between these global integration processes and the processes that code the relations between local parts in the first place.

IMPLEMENTING VISUAL RECOGNITION IN COMPUTERS

We have pointed out some limitations in the Gestalt approach, and highlighted some questions that need to be answered before a full account of visual recognition can be given. Now, one of the most rigorous ways to see how complete a theory is, is to test whether we can implement it in practice. For example, theories of perception may be examined by instructing a computer to carry out the required processes. The theory is supported by the extent to which the computer mimics human perform-ance. When computer implementation is attempted, it soon becomes apparent that theories which simply describe the phenomena at hand are inadequate; we need to be able to quantify the processes involved. For instance, think of the Gestalt principles of grouping as descriptions of how individual form elements combine. For a computer implementation of the principles of grouping we would need to know how close the lines and edges need to be to "group", and how to measure similarity if we are to enable similar forms to group, etc. Consequently, in order to implement a theory researchers often have to go beyond descriptive principles; they have to make quantitative estimates about the processes, and extra assumptions about how the processes inter-relate. Of course, there is a danger in this that many of the assumptions may take us a long way from the original theory; they may take us towards understanding computers rather than human vision. Against this, we may gain new insights into the processes, and their inter-relations, by examining those found necessary when instantiating visual recognition in computers. Given such insights, we must then ask whether the same processes operate in human vision.

To-date, the most complete work on computer vision is probably that conducted by the late David Marr and his colleagues at the Massachusetts Institute of Technology (e.g., Marr, 1976, 1980, 1982; Marr & Hildreth, 1980; Marr & Nishihara, 1978). Marr noted some general points that might apply equally well to human and to computer vision. One such point concerns what he termed the "principle of modular design", which he believed may be necessary to implement complex tasks (such as object recognition) in any information processing system. In such a design the task is sub-divided into separate parts, and the solutions to each part are sought independently of the solutions to other parts. The idea behind this is that, in a modular system, a small change in one process will not precipitate changes in many other processes. In computer programming, modular design is useful for "debugging" purposes, since the programmer can improve one part of a program without altering any other parts. In human vision, modular design might be useful if the processes have different evolutionary or developmental histories, or if they utilise quite different kinds of stimulus information. We might then ask whether some of the processes in human visual recognition are modular.

In at least some respects, the answer here appears to be "yes". We illustrate this point with regard to two aspects of normal human vision that we touched upon in Chapter 1: namely, seeing depth from binocular input and seeing movement.

VISION IN THREE﹒DIMENSIONS

We see objects in three-dimensions (3D), and the ability to judge the depth of objects relative to ourselves is crucial to our negotiations with the world; without this ability we would be much poorer at even apparently simple tasks such as reaching appropriately for objects. Our ability to perceive the depths of objects in 3D is helped by our having two eyes and not just one. Indeed, the advantages to be gained in depth perception probably constitute the main reason both for our having evolved two eyes and for their being positioned in front of and not, say, to the side of the head. Eyes on either side of the head would afford a more panoramic field of view, but less good depth perception: a design characteristic perhaps more suitable for animals which are preyed upon rather than for predators such as man (Walls, 1942). Having two eyes helps in depth perception because information about the depths of objects in 3D can be derived from the degree of difference between the images in the two eyes (their binocular disparity).

One important point here is that binocular disparity information alone can produce depth perception. This was first demonstrated in an ingenious experiment devised by Bela Julesz, now of AT&T Bell Laboratories in New Jersey. Julesz (e.g., Julesz, 1971) produced two copies of a random chequer-board of small black and white dots (see Fig. 3.11a). One patch of the random-dot texture was then shifted horizontally, so that its position differed in the two copies (in the example in Fig. 3.11b, the shifted area is labelled A and its surround S). The copies were then presented simultaneously, one to the left and one to the right eye (a technique termed "stereoscopic viewing"). When this was done, the area that had been shifted to different positions in the two copies appeared to float at a different depth relative to the background. Julesz termed these stimuli "random-dot stereograms".

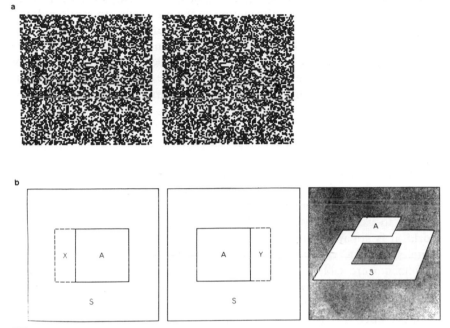

FIG. 3.11.   A random-dot stereogram. Part a gives the members of the stereogram pair. One way to view this pair stereoscopically is to hold a pen about half-way between you and the central point between the two areas of random dots. You shoud initially look at the top of the pen, and then try to shift your attention from the pen to the random dots. With some effort and concentration, the two copies should fuse into one—with the net result being that the area of visual "noise" which has been shifted in the two copies stands out in depth from its background. Should stereoscopic viewing prove difficult by this method, the reader is referred to Frisby (1979) and to Julesz (1971), who present examples where fusion is more easily achieved by printing the two copies of the noise in different colours and providing filtered spectacles so that each copy is presented to only one eye.

Part b shows how the random-dot stereogram is created by shifting one section of noise in the two copies (from Julesz, 1971).

Our normal conscious perception of the visual world is based on information integrated from our two eyes. This integration process enhances our perception of depth by coding disparities between the two retinal images, and by translating these disparities into information about the depths of surfaces relative to the viewer. Random-dot stereograms are important because they produce the impression of two surfaces at different depths, while at the same time there are no cues in either image about what forms the surfaces will take. Stereo viewing of Fig. 3.11a produces the image of a square at a different depth to its background, but there is no information about this square in either the right or the left random-dot patterns. This shows that, in some sense, we are able to see depth independently of the processes involved in seeing form, since even when we reduce monocular form information to the minimum (to random dots), the perception of depth can still occur. Because of this apparent independence of depth perception from form perception, we can think of there being a separate module in the mind, which is devoted to the creation of depth from stereo images, and that this module operates quite independently of the processes involved in perceiving two-dimensional forms.

SEEING MOVEMENT

Normally, our visual world is not composed of static images or of separate snapshots of objects; it is composed of a coherent world in constant motion, either as we move towards or around objects or as objects move relative to us. Yet, if we study how our eyes operate when viewing the world, it is apparent that they dart from place to place, resting only for quite short intervals at particular locations on objects. These short movements are called "saccades", and the periods of rest are termed "fixations". Often we have little awareness that we are making saccades; certainly we are not aware of any blur as we move our eyes, and there is even evidence that the uptake of visual information is suppressed whilst saccades take place (Volkmann, 1976) . It seems that there is more going on here than the simple painting of images onto an inner screen; rather there must be internal processes which integrate the different images together, though quite how this is done remains something of a mystery.

Objects also move relative to us, and when this occurs our eyes can "lock" onto an object, producing what are termed "smooth pursuit" eye movements. It also seems to be the case that information given by the movement of an object can be used for identification purposes. An impressive demonstration of this was devised by the Swedish psychologist, Gunnar Johansson (e.g., Johansson, 1973). An actor was placed in a darkened room and lights were attached to his main joints. When the actor was stationary, the observers only saw a random pattern of lights (Fig. 3.12a). However, as soon as the actor began to walk, it was immediately and vividly apparent that the lights portray a moving human being. Observers can also easily discriminate differences between actors walking and jogging, actors walking with and without a limp, male and female actors etc. (see Johansson, 1975, for an illuminating discussion of this work). Now, the only information that the observer has to go on here is that conveyed by the particular type of movement; there is no consistent pattern to each static image (as only random static images are perceived). Rather like the example of seeing form in depth from random-dot stereograms, Johansson's "moving lights" demonstrate that movement

a   b

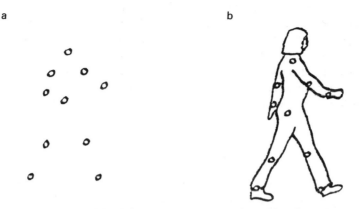

FIG. 3.12. The "moving lights" demonstration. When the subject is stationary, only a random pattern of lights is seen (as in a). When the subject moves, observers report the vivid impression of seeing a person walking (as in b) (from Johansson, 1973).

information alone can give rise to form perception (in this instance, the perception of a moving human being). We might again suggest that the processes involved in using information about the movement patterns of objects are separate from those involved in the perception of static forms, since form can be generated from motion in the absence of static-form cues.

VIEWPOINT-SPECIFIC CODING

The theory that we have outlined proposes that human vision is composed of sets of independent processes (modules), each of which is attempting to solve its own particular problem. It should not go unremarked upon that the functions of the two processing modules we have focused upon, the perception of stereoscopic depth and movement perception, bear more than a passing resemblance to the functions we earlier attributed to some of the different visual areas in the brain (in particular V2 and MT; see Fig. 1.3). Thus there is some convergence between studies of intact human vision, and studies concerned with the preferences of different brain areas for different types of stimulus information. Marr's principle of modularity gives us some insight into why such a modular organisation may be useful.

Marr also made the general point that it is possible to code visual stimuli in various ways, and that these different codings might be needed to support different behaviours. This point is particularly relevant when we come to consider how forms are recognised.

For instance, one purpose of vision is to enable us to manipulate objects in space (to reach for them appropriately, to move around obstructions etc.). Another purpose is to enable objects to be recognised when they are seen from different viewpoints (and therefore when they project different retinal images, at different brightnesses, etc.). Now, in order to guide the manipulation of objects in space visually, a visual system needs to indicate the relations between the object and the perceiver; that is, it needs to preserve information which is specific to the viewpoint from which the object is seen. In contrast, to enable recognition to occur across differing viewpoints, the system needs to use information which is constant to the object irrespective of the viewpoint. Different information is required for these two purposes.

We will deal first with the viewpoint-specific aspects of form perception. Marr's suggestions here are interesting because they align with what we know about how images are initially coded in the brain (Chapter 1, p. 11), though they extend this by considering how the information so coded can be grouped to form perceptual wholes.

Marr proposed that form perception starts by encoding edges in the stimulus. To do this a bank of "edge detectors" is set up, with each detector associated with a particular part of the image. These devices compute the degree of contrast between the intensities of the light at neighbouring points within a specified field, since contrast can be indicative of an edge in the image. Thus these devices are similar to the "edge detector" cells documented by Hubel and Wiesel (see p. 11). However, it was soon realised that if the field associated with each detector device was very small, then a gradual change in light intensity would not be detected. To detect gradual changes in intensity, a larger field must be sampled. However, as larger fields are sampled, information is lost about the precise location of rapid changes in intensity (which could be conveyed by detectors tuned to smaller fields). For this reason, such devices cannot act individually as edge detectors. Marr and Hildreth (1980) therefore proposed that edges were coded by a group of detectors working simultaneously in unison, with the group containing a range of detectors tuned to increasingly larger fields. Accordingly, we can think of a computer (or, to extend our analogy, a brain) sampling an image simultaneously with filters assigned to different spatial regions, and with each region being sampled simultaneously at a number of different spatial scales, from the coarse to the fine. Under most circumstances, an edge signalled by a "fine" detector will also be picked up by "coarser" detectors whose sampling areas include that of the "fine" edge detector. Such coincident activity across a range of detectors is taken as evidence for the presence of an edge in the image. Once an intensity change is detected, then its orientation, spatial extent, position of termination and so forth are coded. On a small number of occasions the signals from "fine" and "coarse" detectors will not coincide, such as when a diffuse shadow is projected onto a sharp edge of an object (here the positions of maximum intensity change picked up by the "fine" and "coarse" detectors, corresponding respectively to the edge of the object and the edges of the shadow, may be at different locations). This non-coincidence can then be taken as evidence for the presence of two different physical phenomena producing intensity changes in the same region of the image but at different spatial scales (in this case, the object projecting the edge and a shadow from another object).

Following the coding of edge information, a second process is undertaken that groups, at each spatial scale, the edges signalled by coincident activity in the detectors, using the Gestalt principles of proximity, similarity and closure.

The above processes of edge detection and grouping serve to build up a picture or description of the edges in an image at different spatial scales. Information about discontinuities between the surfaces of objects, the local depths of the surfaces relative to the viewer, etc., are then added by means of binocular disparity and motion information. Thus the grouping of static-form information is thought to proceed independently of stereoscopic depth perception and movement perception, though each process will contribute to the final description of the object's surfaces relative to the viewer. In this respect, we can see that the process of decomposing an image into its edge components, followed by the embellishment of that coding with depth information, is to recover precise information about the surfaces of the object relative to the viewer. This decomposition is necessary because information about the relative depths of the surfaces of objects is not explicit in the two-dimensional images available on the retina.

Two other points are also worthy of mention. By picking up and comparing edge information at different spatial scales, extra information can be gained about the relations between objects in the world (e.g., whether variations at points in the image are due to a single cause, such as the edge of an object, or to additional causes, such as a shadow across that edge). Also, if information coded on a broad spatial scale becomes available prior to codings of more local relations between edges, then we can see that something like a first-pass process can be implemented. In many respects this first pass will be independent of variation at a more local scale, since information about the precise relations between local edges, for instance, will not be specified.

RECOGNISING FORMS FROM DIFFERENT VIEWS

Unfortunately, the above description of an image cannot be a complete explanation of the mechanisms of object recognition, because the coding of the image would change every time our viewpoint shifted (since edges are coded according to their positions in the field, the coding would change with each position change). Further refinements to the coding are thus likely to be required to enable an object to be recognised from many different viewpoints. For instance, our recognition of objects is strongly influenced by what we take to be their orientation. An "H" can be perceived as an "I" on its side, or, even more dramatically, the silhouette of the dog shown in Fig. 3.13 can be perceived as a chef if the right hand end is taken as the top of the figure (see Rock, 1956, 1973, for further discussion of this point). These examples suggest that recognition involves more than grouping together the parts of an object, it also involves assigning an overall orientation and coding the object in relation to that orientation (e.g., with the right hand line in the "H" being coded as the top line when it is perceived as an "I", etc.). This assignment of orientation may only take place once the locations of intensity change in the image have themselves been coded and grouped. Finally, to enable recognition to take place, the description of the object, taken from its assumed orientation, may be matched against our stored knowledge of the object's form—rather like when we take the title of a book and match it against the titles of books in a library stack. Recognition can be said to take place when a match is found. In terms of our analogy, we might presume that information concerning the meaning of objects, their uses, and our prior associations with them, is contained in the book. By matching the title with the book, we retrieve the book and gain access to this knowledge.

FIG. 3.13.   The ambiguous chef-dog figure (from Rock, 1956).

A SUMMARY

Our discussion has come some way from the simple inner-screen theory of perception we started out with. Studies of how recognition is implemented in the brain show that many different visual areas are implicated, and that different visual areas may perform different jobs. For instance, there seem to be specialist areas for movement and depth perception, and these areas are separate from those concerned with perception of two-dimensional static forms. Static-form perception itself seems to start from the coding of edges in the image.

The notion that vision is highly modular, and that movement, depth, and static-form perception operate independently is also supported by studies of intact human vision and computer vision. Furthermore, even the perception of two-dimensional static forms can be fractionated into a series of separate stages. Such stages may include:

1. the registration of local form elements (such as edges);
2. the coding of the local relations between the form elements (in line with the Gestalt principles);
3. the coding of a global interpretation of an object or scene from local part descriptions (see Figs. 3.9 and 3.10);
4. the assignment of orientation to the object descriptions; and
5. the matching of the final object description against a memory of all known objects.

There remain many unanswered questions concerning the functional relations between these stages of form perception, such as whether the stages are functionally separate so that the operation of one stage has no bearing on the operation of the others. There also remains the question of how such processes are implemented in the brain.

It thus appears that visual recognition is indeed a complex process, and that it is almost certainly dependent on conjoint activity in many brain areas. Nevertheless, it seems possible that damage to areas concerned with the organisation and coding of form could impair visual recognition without affecting other functions, such as stereoscopic depth perception or movement perception. Also, the functions lost in such cases may give us important insights into the nature of the perceptual organisation process itself. With such thoughts in mind, we turn now to a more detailed analysis of John's visual recognition problems.

4 Some Experimental Investigations

In studying John's case, we have tried to consider his problems in terms of the kinds of processes thought to be involved in visual recognition, and which might plausibly be affected by brain damage. Our analysis begins first with a discussion of the type of agnosia involved, before going on to study the particular processes which seem impaired.

VISUAL OBJECT RECOGNITION

John was given a series of standardised line drawings of common objects, and was asked to name them. He found this a far from trivial task, and was correct only on 42% of the instances. He spent a long time coming to his answers, and seemed to be trying to identify the objects by picking out a salient feature rather than by taking the object in "as a whole". For instance, he was able to identify a drawing of a pig by picking out that it had a curly tail. In all cases where he misidentified the object, he responded with the name of another object which bore some visual similarity to the target object. Animals were misidentified as other animals. With other objects, his feature-by-feature descriptions mislead him in quite the wrong direction. For example, when given the drawing of a carrot (Fig. 4.1a) he remarked "I have not even the glimmerings of an idea. The bottom point seems solid and the other bits are feathery. It does not seem to be logical unless it is some sort of a brush." Other errors occurred because he failed to "group" the parts of the object correctly. For instance, he described a drawing of a nose (Fig. 4.1b) as a "soup ladle",

59

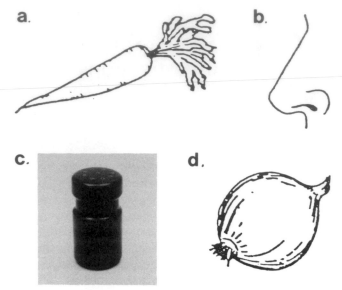

FIG.4.1. Examples of stimuli that John failed to identify correctly: a) line drawing of a carrot; b) line drawing of a nose; c) photograph of a pepper pot; d) line drawing of an onion (line drawings taken from Snodgrass & Vanderwart, 1980—see text for details).

failing to perceive that the inside lines were part of the same object as the outside curved line. Once, when shown the photograph of a paintbrush, he remarked that "It appears to be two things close together; a longish wooden stick and a shorter, darker object, though this can't be right or you would have told me." He also described a photograph of a pepper pot (see Fig. 4.1c) as "A stand containing three separate pans; the top pan has a design on its lid; the second pan has a slightly smaller diameter than the top pan; the bottom pan has a wider diameter than the second pan and is longer in length." With the nose, the paintbrush and the pepper pot, instead of grouping the parts of each object together, he segmented them as if they belonged to different objects.

It is interesting to note that after five years of such tests being conducted at regular intervals, John's ability to recognise line drawings has not altered. In 1981, four months after his stroke, he named a drawing of an onion (Fig. 4.1d) in the following way: "I'm completely lost at the moment. You don't put it on. It has sharp bits at the bottom like a fork. It could be a necklace of sorts." In 1986, when given the same line drawing he said: "It could possibly be an apple, this part would be nearest to the tree (pointing to the roots), this part is too big in relation to the body (pointing to the remains of the leaves)."

From the above example, it might appear that John is inconsistent, in that he misidentifies the onion as two different objects on the two occasions of testing. Inconsistency of response has troubled earlier theorists. In Chapter 1 we mentioned that Eberhard Bay (1952) was so annoyed by the inconsistencies in the behaviour of Goldstein and Gelb's (1918) patient that he proclaimed the patient demented (although Bay did concede that the patient may also have had disturbed "early" visual processes). However, in other respects, John performs very consistently. His overall level of naming of line drawings has remained at the same level over a long testing period, and he also consistently finds some objects more difficult to identify than others, with objects which come from classes where the members tend to look alike being particularly difficult (animals, birds, insects, fruit, and vegetables). The responses he gives may differ on different occasions, but he always tends to misidentify the same objects.

Although John did not score highly in naming line drawings, he was slightly better at naming real objects, scoring about 67% correct. Of course, this might reflect the kinds of objects which can be used for testing—it is not easy to bring a real animal into a laboratory, though it is easy to show a picture of one! However, John remains better at naming real objects even when you use the same objects in both circumstances. Why should real objects prove easier? The best bet here would be that there is simply more information in a real object to aid identification. For instance, information about the size of the object is given when it is real, while it must be inferred from a picture; also in real objects there is disparity information providing cues to the relative depths of surfaces, while such cues are absent in two-dimensional line drawings. Interestingly, over time, John's ability to use such cues appears to have improved. In 1986 he was tested with the same real objects as previously and this time scored 85% correct. Though this is still poor compared with the 100% correct recognition we would normally expect for common everyday objects, it does represent a real improvement. Yet his basic visual processing, to gauge from his performance with line drawings, had not improved. Thus John seems to have developed strategies for using the extra information available in real objects to help overcome his residual deficit.

Although John was poor at identifying objects from vision, he could manage a great deal better if he was allowed to touch the object. For this test, John, to his consternation, was blindfolded and an object was placed in his hands. He was allowed to feel the object for as long as he liked, and then he had to name it. At the time he scored 67% correct on identifying real objects from vision, he scored 85% correct on the same objects from touch. This finding establishes that his recognition problem was specific to vision, and that it was not a general naming problem.

FACE RECOGNITION

John's recognition problem was not confined to objects, he could also not recognise people from their faces. This was brought home to us quite dramatically on one occasion. After some months of quite intensive testing we called unexpectedly at his home one snowy evening and John opened the door. "Hello", we said, and then quickly realised that he had absolutely no idea who we were, and initially he mistook us to be cousins of his wife. This was quite different to our usual meetings, where he expected our visit and greeted us socially and, to all intents and purposes, normally on our arrival. On this occasion, however, his blank look of complete non-identification indicated just how profound his problem was.

We conducted some tests to examine his face recognition. In one we gave him three photographs of faces, one of which was the face of a famous person, the others were of undergraduates from the University who would be unknown to him. His task was to pick out, and if possible also name, the famous face. He failed to get any correct, though control subjects scored 100%. We then picked out the famous faces and asked him to name them. His naming responses were often a long way off the mark. For instance, he said Winston Churchill was a woman because, in the picture we used, he did not wear a tie. Jackie Stewart (the racing driver) was also identified as a female because he had long hair. He also fared no better when asked to classify famous faces as either politicians or royalty. The Queen, the Duke of Edinburgh, Prince Charles and Princess Anne were all classed as politicians, whilst Edward Heath and Harold Wilson were classed as royalty! When we read the names to him, though, this classification task was trivially easy.

IS IT A RECOGNITION OR A NAMING PROBLEM?

Indubitably John has a problem in naming visually presented objects, but is it just a naming problem or is it a problem with recognition—does he actually not know anything about the objects or people he fails to identify, rather than just failing to recall their names? We have all been in situations where we know we can recognise an object or person, but just can't think of the name. Perhaps John just has some exaggerated version of this problem. Against this, his performance on our tests of face recognition suggests that he actually doesn't recognise the people when he misidentifies them, after all, the tests just required the people to be categorised (as famous or as politicians), and it ought to be possible to do this even if the name has slipped our mind for the time being. We conducted similar categorisation tests to assess his recognition of objects. He was given three photographs of objects, two of which were different exemplars of the same kind of object (such as two kinds of pepper pot, a grinder, and a shaker), and the other was a different object which happened to look like one of the target objects. John was simply asked to point to the two photographs which showed the same kinds of object. In a similar way to his performance on the test of face recognition, John was relatively poor at this object-matching task. Yet he can perform very well (in fact better than age-matched control subjects) when asked to match photographs of exactly the same object, but portrayed from two different points of view. This he does by matching salient features of the object in the two photographs, so that when the object is rotated to hide such features he is relatively disrupted (Humphreys & Riddoch, 1984). Thus he can do certain types of matching task—in particular, he can match visual features in two photographs. He is only particularly impaired when the task requires him to *recognise* the objects.

IS THERE A PROBLEM WITH VISUAL SENSATION OR INTELLECT?

Given this general background, we can begin to ask how John fits in with the various types of agnosia. We also need to ask whether John truly has a recognition disorder, or whether his problems are caused by some residual deficit in his visual sensation or his intellect, or some combination of the two (as Bay, 1953, suggested; see Chapter 1, p. 20). We turn to the last question first.

On meeting John socially, one is struck by the normality of his behaviour and it is consequently difficult for his friends and acquaintances to realise the extent of his recognition problems. He is able to hold his own in discussions and conversations as well as he did before having a stroke, he is able to reach correctly for objects, he can shake hands appropriately etc. It is only when he is required to recognise the objects or the people he encounters that his behaviour can seem bizarre. However, even when he makes identification errors, he retains the capacity to cope—as revealed by his contingency plans in the event of his being lost (Chapter 2). One would certainly not think that this was a person with a lowered intellect or with some form of progressive dementia.

John's knowledge about objects and events was tested by asking him to give verbal definitions about objects that he is typically unable to identify. On such occasions, he attempted to give as near to the dictionary definitions as he could. As we can see from the examples in Fig. 4.2, his definitions are extremely detailed and a pleasure to read.

Such definitions confirm one's initial impression of John; he has good

GOAT
John's definition: "A four legged domesticated animal usually kept for its milk (in Europe) but can also be kept for its meat (in the near-East). It has a fairly extended neck and head, whose features vary according to type; however, the features would include extended ears and horns on the male. It is white in colour. It eats rough vegetation. Size between two and three feet high."

John's object naming: "An animal, I suppose it could be a cow."

CARROT
John's definition: "A carrot is a root vegetable cultivated and eaten as human consumption worldwide. Grown from seed as an annual crop, the carrot produces long thin leaves growing from a root head; this is deep growing and large in comparison with the leaf growth, sometimes gaining a length of 12 inches under a leaf top of similar height when grown in good soil. Carrots may be eaten raw or cooked and can be harvested during any size or state of growth. The general shape of a carrot root is an elongated cone and its colour ranges between red and yellow."

John's object naming: "A brush."

LETTUCE
John's definition: "A lettuce is a quick growing, annual plant, cultivated for human consumption of its succulent, crisp green leaves which grow, during the young stage of the plant, tightly formed together in a general ball-shaped mass.

Widely cultivated, lettuces are of many varieties and of absolutely no value as a food. They do, however, enable one to eat delicious mayonnaise when using a knife and fork in polite places."

John's object naming: "Is this a real thing? A ball of paper?"

NAIL
John's definition: "First, this is a pin-shaped, sharp-pointed, thin cone of metal, with one end expanded and flattened to form a head-piece, to provide the striking point for a hammer to drive the nail into timber. Second, nails are the hard, sharp-edged ends of human fingers and toes."

John's object naming: "A pencil."

FIG. 4.2.   Examples of John's definitions of objects he typically fails to identify from vision. Examples of his visual misidentifications are also given.

knowledge about the objects that he fails to recognise, and he is well able to articulate this knowledge. However, it is almost inevitable that in giving verbal definitions about objects we tend to stress what we do with them and the things they are used with, rather than what they look like. That is, we tend to stress their functions rather than their visual attributes. This was also true of John's definitions, although, in some instances, he did give rather precise information about the object's visual characteristics (see Fig. 4.2). Now, while John's verbal definitions clearly refute the idea that he has generally impaired intellectual functions, they do not prove that his agnosia is due to something other than a loss of knowledge about objects. This is because we can distinguish between our knowledge about visual attributes of objects and our verbal knowledge about their functions. Indeed, there are intriguing cases in the neurological literature where patients seem to have both visual and verbal knowledge about objects, but somehow can't link the two together. Beauvois (1982; Beauvois & Saillant, 1985) reports the case of a patient who knew that "snow" was linked with "white" from the story "Snow White"—this can be termed "verbal knowledge" because it is learned as a verbal phrase. The patient also knew whether the snow in the picture of a hillside was correctly coloured, indicating intact visual knowledge. But, if asked to name the colour of snow in a picture she would often give the wrong name. She was unable to go from her visual knowledge, that the snow was correctly coloured, to her verbal knowledge concerning the label for that colour. From this, we might suspect that "visual knowledge" and "verbal knowledge" about the functions of objects are stored in different areas of the brain. A patient may have very good verbal knowledge but still be unable to recognise objects because his or her visual knowledge has been disrupted.

To assess John's visual knowledge about objects, we asked him to draw a set of 76 objects from memory. This set included various animals, birds, insects, fruits and vegetables—the very objects he typically misidentifies. Nobody, unless they are artistically inclined, finds it easy to draw items from memory—particularly items from the above classes. Given this fact, John's drawings are very good, and somewhat better than the more modest attempts of one of the present authors! Examples are given in Fig. 4.3.

On other occasions we presented John with "incomplete" line drawings, where we erased some feature of the object. He was than asked to complete the drawings. If he was able to identify the object, he was able to draw in the missing part. He was unable to complete any of the drawings where he failed to identify the object. Later we told him the identities of these objects, and he was then able to complete the figures appropriately. Fig. 4.4a shows his attempt to complete the drawing of an elephant, which he had failed to identify (he could only name it as an animal), and Fig. 4.4b his attempt when he was told what it was. These tests indicate that he does

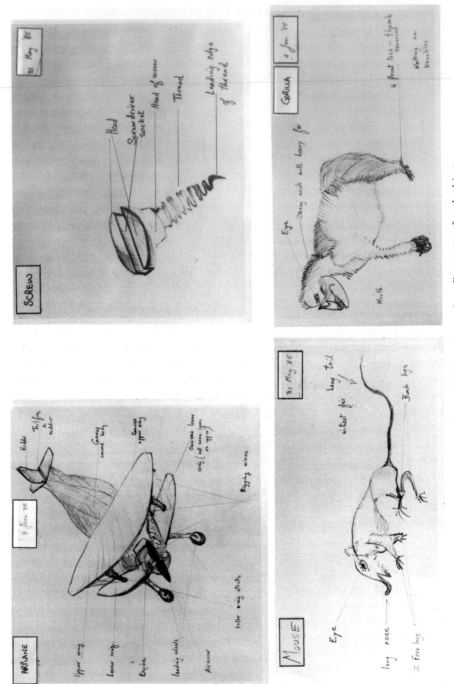

FIG. 4.3   Examples of John's drawings from memory, along with his notes on the salient parts of each objects.

FIG. 4.4. Examples of John's "completion of drawings": a) shows his completion of an elephant after failing to identify the animal from the drawing; b) shows his completion of the drawing once he was told what it depicted.

have stored knowledge about what objects look like, so loss of this knowledge cannot be the reason for his agnosia.

If it cannot be argued that John's stored knowledge and intellect have been damaged, does he have some residual impairment in sensation? As we noted in Chapter 2, quite extensive examinations of John's "visual fields" have been undertaken, with consistent results: John has a "superior altitudinal field defect", which prevents his seeing any input from the top halves of both his visual fields. In contrast, his detection of light in the lower halves of both fields is essentially normal. This field defect alone cannot account for his poor recognition, since he fails to recognise objects even when they are presented to the intact parts of his visual fields (see Chapter 2).

Other types of impairment in visual sensation are possible. One might occur if John has a problem in moving his eyes appropriately around objects as he inspects them. In Chapter 3 (p. 52), we discussed how our eyes are never stationary for long, and how our views of a scene are composed of periods of fixation interspersed by short saccadic eye movements. It is possible that a patient may have a problem in controlling and guiding his or her eye movements, or the patient may fail to fixate correctly. Such problems would result in inappropriate retinal images being formed, which may not allow accurate recognition to occur.

A possible relation between abnormal eye movement patterns and recognition disorders was noted by the eminent Russian neurologist, Aleksandr Romanovich Luria (1973). As early as 1909, Balint, another neurologist, had described a patient who appeared able to recognise only one object at a time: a defect termed simultanagnosia (meaning a problem in the recognition of simultaneously presented objects). This patient also showed disordered patterns of eye movements. Such disordered eye movements may occur if the patient cannot process input from distant locations simultaneously, and so cannot direct their eyes to a new location from the place where they are fixating. Luria suggested that, in at least some cases of agnosia, the spatial range over which information may be processed simultaneously may be even more restricted, so that even the recognition of single objects is impaired. The effect of this would be something akin to extreme tunnel vision, a proposal also made by Bay (1950, 1953), though for different reasons (remember that Bay argued that vision would be constricted by the rapid fading of visual information, rather than the inability to process information from different locations simultaneously; Chapter 1, p. 20). If vision in agnosic patients is constricted in this way it would not be picked up by standard tests of the visual fields, since such tests present single lights, whereas lights in two or more locations would need to appear simultaneously for a deficit to show. Now, such a marked deficit in simultaneous processing of visual information should also hinder the patient's eye movements, so one would expect the recognition disorder to be accompanied by very abnormal eye movement patterns.

In our interactions with John we were unable to discern any problems in his control of eye movements. John's eye movements were subsequently studied more carefully by Dr. Chris Kennard and Dr. Trevor Crawford of The London Hospital, who recorded his eye-movement patterns. Saccades were required to lights which appeared at random first along a horizontal line and then in a vertical line, and his ability to track a smoothly-moving target (smooth-pursuit movements) were also assessed. The patterns of eye movements were essentially normal, though John had to compensate when targets appeared at random in his blind (upper) fields by moving his eyes upwards in small steps until the target was found.

It seems that John's problem in visual recognition cannot be attributed to a visual field defect or to his having disordered patterns of eye movements, and on pages 72–79 we go on to present evidence which directly refutes the idea that his vision is spatially restricted, contrary to the suggestions of both Bay and Luria. John also retains extensive knowledge about the objects he can no longer identify visually. His recognition disorder is not due to decreased intellect.

TYPES OF VISUAL AGNOSIA

John does not have deficient stored knowledge either about what objects look like, or about their functions and his prior associations with them. His

FIG 4.5. Example of John's copy of a line drawing of an owl.

problem does not seem to be due to the loss of stored information about objects.

Early on in our testing of John, we also established that he could provide accurate copies of objects—even when he had no idea what the object was. This is illustrated by his copy of the picture of an owl (Fig. 4.5). In the picture, part of the owl's left eye is missing. Normally, having knowledge that an owl is represented by the drawing, we would tend to draw in and "complete" the missing part. In contrast, John faithfully reproduced the gap in the drawing—if anything, making it proportionally larger than in the original. When copying this picture, he stated that all he saw was a complex pattern of lines, which did not correspond to a particular object. The failure to identify the object is apparent in his drawing.

John's drawing of an owl also illustrates the very painstaking line-by-line copying strategy he used—were this not so, we might again expect completion to occur. This copying strategy has remained constant since his lesion. Recently we asked him to copy a lithograph of St. Paul's Cathedral, London, which hangs in his living room and which is a long-time favourite picture (see Chapter 3). This copy is shown in Fig. 4.6. It is an accurate representation of the original, but it took six hours to complete!

However, whilst John copies accurately, it would be incorrect to say that he copies "normally"—copying is a slow, effortful process for him. The painstaking line-by-line strategy he uses to copy is similar to the feature-by-feature descriptions he gives when trying to identify objects.

One interpretation of these two characteristics of his performance is that John has intact registration of form elements (single lines and edges), but that his ability to integrate these elements into "perceptual wholes" is in some way impaired. The intact information about the local form elements enables him to make accurate copies of stimuli he cannot identify. However, he copies in a slow and slavish manner because his perceptual representations of the stimuli are not correctly organised and

FIG. 4.6.   John's copy of an etching of St. Paul's cathedral, London.

integrated. Similarly, his object identification may be based on feature-by-feature descriptions because he only has available information about individual form elements. Normally, when we copy a picture, we might first sketch its overall shape and then "fill in" the details. This filling-in process can be influenced by information about the overall form. For instance, we find it more difficult to copy an "impossible" figure (such as the triangle in Fig. 3.10) than their possible equivalents (e.g., a triangle with normal depth relations between its three corners), presumably because information about the "whole" is consistent with that of the parts in "possible" figures. Now, a patient using unintegrated information about form may not use this strategy; rather they may faithfully reproduce a gap in the figure because the information about the overall form is not available to "drive" the filling-in process. We can thus conceptualise John's copy of the owl as a failure in this filling-in process.

Interestingly, other investigators have remarked that the agnosic patients they worked with produced accurate but slavish copies of objects (e.g., Ratcliff & Newcombe, 1982). Ratcliff (1985) also reported that the patient he studied showed no advantage when copying "possible" over "impossible" figures. This is consistent with the idea that the patient failed to use information about the "whole" object to guide the drawing of its parts. In some cases, a line-by-line copying strategy is accompanied by a problem in "keeping one's place". Levine's (1978) patient complained that she lost her place "when she raised her pencil from the drawing surface." The "artistic" patient described by Wapner et al. (1978, see p. 19) was able to generate copies of objects which were generally accurate and maintained some of the characteristics of his former artistic skill; however, he also lost his place on occasions, with the result that bits were left out (for example, the nose of an aeroplane, the receiver of a telephone) or that certain aspects were repeated (resulting in a five-legged rhinocerous, an accordian with three keyboards, and an aeroplane with a multitude of propellors). John does not show this tendency, and he does not miss or duplicate parts. Thus, it appears that these other patients had additional problems in keeping their place, and that such problems do not necessarily occur with line-by-line copying. We should also note here that John's ability to keep his place could not so readily occur if he had disordered eye movements (see Luria, 1973).

According to this analysis John does not have the same "apperceptive" problems as the patient described by, for instance, Benson and Greenberg (1969), as John appears to have accurate perception of individual form elements. Nevertheless, John does seem to have a subtle impairment to his perceptual processes, which forces him to use a line-by-line copying strategy and a feature-by-feature identification strategy. We suggest that both strategies stem from a difficulty in integrating local form elements into perceptual wholes.

Our diagnosis of John was supported by various other findings. For instance, we found that his ability to identify visual stimuli was greatly impaired if the stimuli were positioned to overlap each other, (see Fig. 4.7), with the disruption caused by overlapping the figures being about ten times that found in control subjects. This disruption occurred whether the stimuli were geometrical figures, letters or line drawings of objects, and when the stimuli were chosen so that John could identify them all when shown in isolation. John has a problem with overlapping figures because he finds it difficult to group individual line segments together; consequently, he often does not know which line goes with which object. This problem is exemplified by his responses to triplets of overlapping letters (Fig. 4.7). Whereas most people identify these triplets by working through the forms in one direction (e.g. "A", "B", "C"), John had to identify each outside letter first before working back to identify the inner letter by way of elimination.

John was also strongly affected when the stimuli were shown for a brief duration. Normally, we can identify pictures of objects even from very brief glimpses lasting no more than a tenth of a second. At such a short presentation rate, John can identify very few pictures correctly. What happens then is that there is an exaggeration of his tendency to identify the general class of objects at the expense of knowing their specific identities. He is even more likely than usual to identify a dog as being just some form of animal. The strong effects of shortened exposure times are consistent with the idea that John codes the detailed features of objects abnormally slowly, and so is detrimentally affected when the object is removed before

FIG. 4.7. Example of overlapping letters.

this coding can be completed. John's problem relates to the processes which combine the local parts of objects to provide an elaborated perceptual whole.

WHAT GOES WRONG IN SUCH CASES?

The brain lesion that John has suffered appears to have selectively impaired his ability to code and group individual form elements. In a sense, this brings to a close the first part of our investigations. However, if we wish to understand his problem fully, and if we are to draw any implications for normal vision from the case, further questions must be asked.

For instance, in his everyday behaviour John seems to have at least some kinds of "global" information about the overall shape of objects. He does not bump into obstacles, he can reach appropriately to pick up an object or to shake hands etc. He does not seem to live in a world composed only of disjointed edges, rather he reports that the world seems "out of focus to the brain"—even though it is not out of focus, in the sense that he has normal acuity (corrected with spectacles) and he can perceive single lines and edges perfectly accurately. What is the relation between the "global" information he appears to have about objects and his problem in grouping individual form elements? This question is relevant not only to understanding the nature of John's visual recognition defect, it is also relevant to understanding the relations between perceptual wholes and their parts in normal recognition (see Chapter 4, pp. 44–49).

We have examined the issue in various ways. To begin with, we queried whether John really did have "global" form information available. A simple task was devised: John was given a set of cards, half of which had a picture of a common object drawn on them. The other half had "new" objects which we created by transposing the parts from two real objects (c.g., such as replacing the tail of a kangaroo with a foot, see Fig. 4.8). John just had to sort the cards into two piles, one of real objects and one of "new" objects. We did this test twice, once with line drawings of new and real objects, and once with their silhouettes. The idea here was as follows: if John has "global" form information available, he may be able to distinguish the real and the new objects from their silhouettes—because only the global outline of the object is then visible. On the other hand, we suspected that he would find the line drawings rather more difficult since he

OBJECT DECISION TASK
a. Line drawings

b. Silhouettes

FIG. 4.8.   Examples of the novel stimuli we created by transposing "parts" from different objects: a) the line drawing version; b) the silhouette version.

tends to "fix" on the local parts of such drawings in an attempt to identify the object. It is as if he cannot help using the internal details in such drawings, even though he is impaired at doing so and even though these details may lead him to group different parts of the drawing incorrectly. This turned out to be the case. John was better at the "real object—new object" task with silhouettes than with line drawings. The result is interesting because control subjects do exactly the opposite; they find the line drawings easier than silhouettes. It appears that, normally, we group the local details in line drawings correctly and such details add further information to help distinguish the stimuli. John, however, does not group the details correctly and they actually get in the way of his using the shape outlines. The "real object–new object" task indicated that John can code global form information. It seems unlikely that this could occur if he had some form of "tunnel vision" (c.f., Bay, 1953; and Chapter 2, p. 20).

Other experiments examined in more detail the relations between his coding of "part" and "whole" forms. In one set of experiments he was given a simple detection or "visual search" task. Various stimuli were presented on a T.V. screen by means of a microcomputer, and he was asked to decide if a particular target was present. By varying the relationship between the target and other "distractor" stimuli, we can assess the kinds of discriminations that John is capable of making. First, he was asked to decide if a target line at a tangent of 45° was present ($\searrow$) against a background of upright distractors (|). This tested his ability to make discriminations based on orientation information (see Fig. 4.9a). John performed quite normally. His reaction times were as quick as control subjects, and his performance was not affected by the number of distractors present: he was as quick when there were nine distractors as when there was one. This confirms our conclusion from his line drawings: John's processing of single lines is intact. It also shows that he can process single lines simultaneously at different locations; if he were only able to process one line at a time, it would take him longer to find the target when there were nine distractors than when there was one.

We then made a small change to the task. Instead of having to detect a single line at a different orientation to the background, John was asked to detect a combination of two lines at two orientations. The target was an inverted "T" ($\perp$) and the distractors were upright "T"s. The targets and distractors in this case differ only in the combination of their horizontal and vertical line components (Fig. 4.9b). One might imagine that this change would not make a great deal of difference. Indeed, control subjects do not find it a difficult task, though one interesting point is that they find it particularly easy to decide when the target is absent; it is as if they perceive that the display as a whole is composed of a homogeneous group of "T"s.

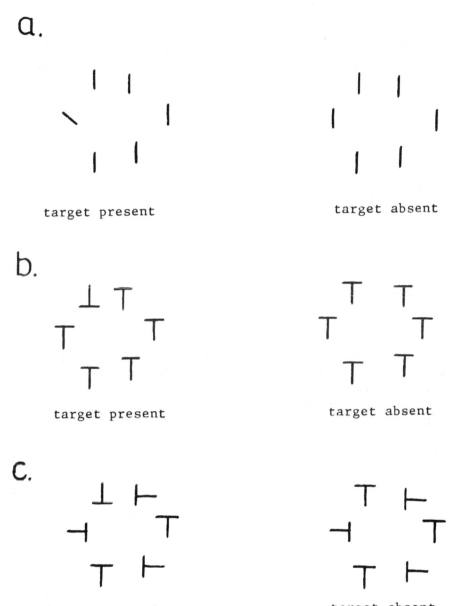

FIG. 4.9. Examples of displays from the visual search tasks (only "regular" displays are shown): a) the subject has to decide whether a sloping line is present; b) the subject has to decide whether an inverted "T" ($\perp$) is present; with homogeneous distractors; c) the subject has to decide whether an inverted "T" is present with heterogeneous distractors.

In contrast, John found this quite a difficult task. He had to search each item in the display, one at a time, to decide whether or not each was the target. This meant that he was quicker to decide that a target was present than when it was absent, since he had to search all the items before he could respond that the target was absent, whilst, on average, he only had to search half to find it when it was present. This pattern of performance remained essentially unchanged even when we gave him up to 3,000 trials! John's search for a combination of features differs *qualitatively* from the control subjects. This difference seems to occur because, while control subjects can combine features simultaneously at different spatial locations (to perceive the homogeneous group of "T"s), John cannot. For John, the process of "binding" individual features together seems to be effortful, and to only occur at one location at a time.

Now, given that John had to search each item in the display one at a time, it was interesting to note that his responses were quicker if the items formed a regular pattern than if they were scattered at random in the field. There seems to be a paradox here. Apparently, John was able to process the items simultaneously to know whether they formed a regular pattern, yet he was unable to combine the individual features of the items simultaneously. However, this is only a paradox if one believes that our perception of a global regular pattern is built on the same processes as our perception of particular combinations of form features (as T or ⊥). In fact, John's ability to perceive the global pattern whilst being massively impaired at "binding" the features together, indicates that there are different processes involved. Our perception of the global pattern depends only on the locations of the items, whilst "binding" the features together requires detailed coding of their brightness, size, length, orientation etc. These processes appear to take place in different areas of the brain. We may speculate that location coding is performed via the occipital-parietal lobe pathway which appears to be intact in John, whilst "feature-binding" is performed via the occipital-temporal lobe pathway (see Fig. 1.3, Chapter 1). In John we seem to see a dissociation between a "first pass" process where the locations of form elements are coded (as in the global patterns), and a more detailed coding of the relations between individual form elements. His case provides grounds for arguing that both "first pass" and detailed codings occur during perception, and that the "first pass" coding can operate independently of the more detailed coding processes. His case thus helps to answer some of the questions we raised when considering the limitations of the Gestalt approach (Chapter 4, p. 46).

Before we accept this conclusion, however, a note of caution might be sounded. Perhaps John's problem is not just concerned with "binding" local features together; perhaps he simply has slower or less accurate or just generally worse visual processes, which impair his performance whenever the task becomes more difficult. Discriminating ⊥ from "T", in the last experiment, was more difficult than discriminating ＼ from │ (in the first visual search experiment). Perhaps task difficulty is more important than anything else. This is certainly something which should be borne in mind when considering such cases. However, we do not believe it to be crucial here. This may be illustrated by another visual search experiment, where we asked John to detect an inverted "T" target again (⊥), but this time against a background of "T"s at various orientations (⊢) and (⊣). In this task, subjects can no longer respond on the basis of homogeneous distractors, since the distractors are a heterogeneous set of "T"s at different orientations. Because of this, the task is much more difficult than the above search tasks, and even control subjects have to search each item in the display one at a time to detect the target (see Fig. 4.9c). Thus they check each feature combination in a slow and effortful way. One might imagine that because the task is difficult for the controls, it would be especially difficult for John. But this was not so. John performed just like the control subjects; indeed, his search rate was quicker, if anything. This confirms that John's vision is selectively affected; it is not in some way simply "worse" than normal vision. Tasks that are quite easy for us are difficult for him, whilst tasks that are difficult for us are not especially difficult for him. What differentiates the tasks is the processes involved, not their level of difficulty. "Search processes" in John are not impaired *per se*; what is impaired is the ability to combine individual features simultaneously at different locations, so that he is unable to take advantage of the homogeneity of these feature combinations when it is available (in the ⊥ vs T task).

A final experiment we conducted helps to throw some further light on the circumstances when John finds feature combinations difficult. He was presented with large "global" letters made up of smaller "local" letters (see Fig. 4.10). On one occasion he was asked to identify the global letters, on another he was asked to identify the local letters, and his response times were recorded. Normally, we are faster at identifying the global letters. When we originally carried out this experiment with John, we thought he might have to identify the letters "feature-by-feature", so that he might respond faster to the local than to the global letters. To our initial chagrin, he responded faster to the global letters. In fact, his responses to the global letters were indistinguishable from the responses of the control subjects. However, his responses to the local letters were abnormally slow. If the local letters were placed individually in the same field locations, his response times improved dramatically and came back into the normal range. What seems to be going on here is that when the local letters are part of a "perceptual whole" (the global letter), John is poor at segmenting them appropriately—that is, he finds it difficult to treat each letter as a

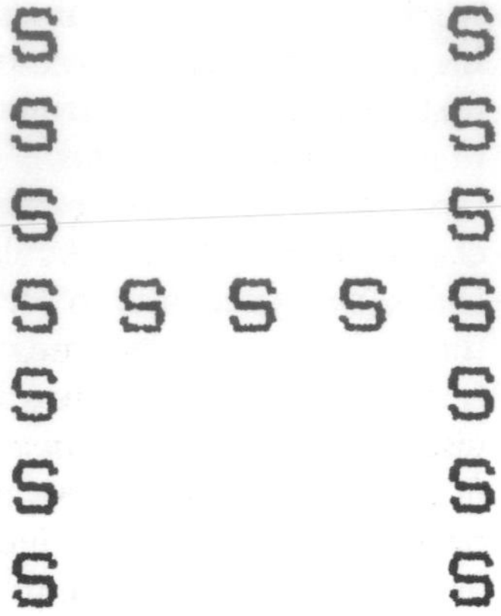

```
S                    S
S                    S
S                    S
S  S  S  S  S
S                    S
S                    S
S                    S
```

FIG. 4.10.   A global letter (H) composed
of smaller, local letters (Ss).

separate object. There seems to be abnormal "cross-talk" between the individual letters, impairing their identification *en masse*. We are reminded here of John's own comment concerning situations where he "cannot see the trees for the wood." This seems to be a precise description of his performance in this last experiment. The problem again appears to reflect impaired grouping processes, in which he finds it difficult to assign lines to their appropriate relative locations; but, in this case, the experiment shows that the problem is exacerbated by placing the "to-be-grouped" elements in close spatial positions. This problem does not seem to affect his responses to the global forms, though, which again illustrates that "first pass" coding of an object's overall shape can be relatively independent of the more detailed coding of its parts.

From these experiments we can make some inferences about John's "visual world". Clearly, he does appear to have global information about the shape of objects. This enables him to move around objects, to grasp them and lift them etc. The information also enables him to recognise the general class that the object belongs to—so that he knows when he is looking at a face, an animal, a car or even a plane (see Chapter 3). However, by itself, this global information is not sufficient for him to be able to identify the owner of the face, or the particular animal, car or plane accurately. For accurate identification of particular exemplars of these classes, this global information must be elaborated. For instance, it must include detailed coding about the visual characteristics of the "parts" of the object, and about their interrelations. Also, this detailed coding probably needs to be elaborated so that it coincides with the global shape information. It is just this detailed coding function that we believe is impaired in John. This may mean that his world is composed of rather gross descriptions of objects—the kinds of descriptions we might make if we glimpsed objects from the corner of an eye. In this respect, he appears to be correct when he says that the world "seems out of focus to the brain," Yet, in another sense, it is not out of focus. He can code the detailed relations between individual shape elements, but it is a slow, effortful process, and it seems to operate on one group of features at a time. Consequently, he is unable to build up a complete picture of both the overall object and the relations between the parts at the same time. Indeed, once he tries to code the relations between the parts of objects, it seems likely that he loses the picture of the whole, so he is left with fragmented information which makes little sense. The picture of John's visual world, that we can construct from our experimental tests, seems to fit fairly well with his own introspections. Consider his descriptions of his own face in the mirror, which he sees either as an unfamiliar "global" face, or as sets of unrelated details (hairline, scar on the nose, etc.—see Chapter 3). This is just what we might expect if there is dissociation between his "global" information about objects and the detailed coding of their parts.

OTHER QUESTIONS

In Chapter 4 we introduced the notion, derived from the Gestalt psychologists, that visual recognition is based on the internal coding and organisation of visual information. We also discussed some limitations in the Gestalt approach (pp. 41–44 and 44–49, Chapter 3). The recognition impairment sustained by John is directly relevant to these limitations. For instance, one limitation concerned the failure of the Gestalt psychologists to specify the relations between perceptual wholes and their parts. John's case, however, suggests that information about perceptual wholes can be derived independently of detailed coding about the parts, since he is impaired at only the latter process (pp. 72–79).

His case is also relevant to the question of how, having coded the relations between lines and edges at one location, we integrate this coding with other locally-based codings to form a global interpretation of a scene. Logically, the global integration process is separate from that of coding the relations between the lines and edges at each location in the first place. The question is, are these two processes differentiated for John? Is John able to integrate local codings into a global interpretation of a scene, despite being impaired at "binding the features" to begin with?

We asked John to make comments about the Hogarth etching and the ambiguous triangle, shown in Figs. 3.9 and 3.10. Although he took some time to assimilate each picture, he was aware of the ambiguities present in both instances. Thus, in describing the Hogarth etching he stated that the "rod held by the eighteenth-century gentleman is ridiculous since it reaches too far, right over to the horse and cart." He also commented that the "triangle doesn't make sense, the corners could never be made to fit together in the way its shown." These descriptions suggest that he is able to link his coding of the parts of objects or scenes together to form a global interpretation. John's case demonstrates that this linking process is independent of the processes concerned with combining the local features in the first place.

Another limitation we noted with the Gestalt approach was that it did not consider the circumstances when perceptual wholes influence the recognition of the parts. We have already argued that John can derive "global" information about objects even though the simultaneous coding of their parts is disrupted. Can this global information sometimes influence the processing of the parts, and, if so, how does this occur?

It is undoubtedly true that "context" exerts a great influence on John's recognition of objects. This is illustrated even by his description of the Hogarth etching, since he typically has enormous difficulty recognising a horse if it is seen in isolation. Might the whole scene here influence his representation of the objects? For instance, might the scene help him to organise the visual information appropriately to "see" the horse, whereas in isolation this would not normally occur? We were able to show that John's ability to identify objects improved when the objects were in an appropriate context. We gave him a set of line drawings along with a drawing of a scene to which each belonged (Fig. 4.11a). He was able to name only about 25% of the drawings in isolation, but about 70% when the contextual scenes were also given. From this, one might conclude that the scenes do help him organise the visual information he receives, improving his visual recognition. Unfortunately, another test showed that this conclusion is probably unwarranted. We repeated the "scene context" experiment, but this time gave him two line drawings of objects which looked alike, along with a scene which was appropriate to only one of the objects (Fig. 4.11b). He was asked to decide which of the two objects was appropriate to the scene, and then he had to name it. In this case, he only named about 40% of the single objects—not much better than when the objects were seen in isolation. When he misidentified objects, he tried to interpret them to fit the scene. For instance, when asked to choose whether the telephone or the petrol pump fitted the garage scene (Fig. 4.11), he chose the telephone, which he proceeded to name as an oil can. This suggests that scene contexts do not change John's perception in any fundamental way; they do not help him to organise information so that he "sees" objects differently. Rather, the contexts seem to bias the kinds of interpretations he gives to objects. In a sense, John is rather in the position that we might be when looking at a camouflaged figure, such as that shown in Fig. 3.6. We find it difficult to identify the object in this figure because we cannot separate the "figure" from the "ground". However, once we are

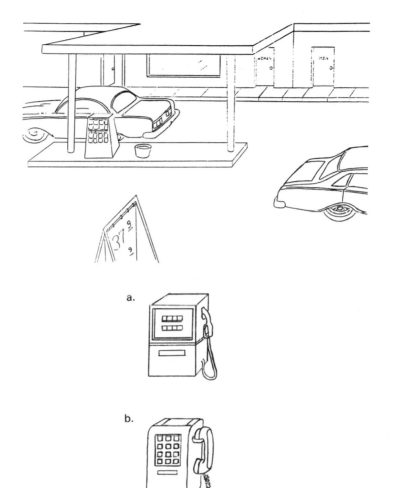

a.

b.

FIG. 4.11.   Examples of stimuli used to examine the effects of contextual scenes on John's ability to identify line drawings: a) shows an object with its appropriate context; b) shows the visually similar distractor to the target object in (a) (from Palmer, 1975/b).

told that it is a picture of a frog against a tree trunk, the correct organisation may fall into place, and we may then find it difficult to imagine seeing the picture any other way. Unfortunately for John, this "falling into place" does not seem to occur. Even when he knows the context and the objects that are likely to occur, his recognition still requires a piecemeal process of matching salient parts of the objects with his hypotheses. He is never able to "see" the frog in the way that we do. At least for John, context does not influence form perception, only the process of assigning responses to what remain impaired perceptions.

5 Other Visual Problems in Agnosic Patients

So far, we have stressed that the primary deficit of visual object recognition is the defining criterion for visual agnosia. However, it is also true that agnosic patients often have deficits in other visual functions, such as colour perception, finding their way, recognising faces, reading, and their visual memory for stimuli and events. A relevant question here is whether these ancillary deficits occur in all agnosic patients, or whether they are specific to particular types of agnosia. Further, in cases where the deficits co-occur, we might ask whether they are all due to a deficit in a single process or whether the patient has multiple, different, deficits. Multiple different deficits might result if the patient has suffered more than one brain lesion or if a given lesion affects more than one process. To answer these questions, we must consider each ancillary deficit in turn. First, we consider these deficits in previous cases in the literature; we then consider whether John also has these visual functions impaired.

LOSS OF COLOUR VISION—ACHROMATOPSIA

In Chapter 1 we discussed cases where insult to the brain produces a complete loss of colour vision, termed achromatopsia. In that discussion we noted that achromatopsia is associated with disorders in recognising complex visual stimuli, such as faces. In a similar way, disorders of visual recognition are also often associated with achromatopsia.

In some cases, the loss of colour perception appears to detract from the quality of life. For instance, the agnosic patient reported by Bornstein and

Kidron (1959) stated that: "Everything I see appears grey and the sky always appears cloudy. The sun looks dirty to me." What is more, the loss of colour vision may substantially augment the patient's recognition problems, as may be seen in comments made by Pallis's (1955) patient: "Everything appears in various shades of grey. My shirts all look dirty and I can't tell one of them from the other. I have no idea which tie to wear. . . . I can't tell whether the light in a room is on or off and from a distance I don't know if a fire is burning or not. . . . I have difficulty in recognising certain foods on my plate until I have tasted or smelled them. I can tell peas or bananas from their size and shape. An omlette, however, looks like a piece of meat and when I open a jar I never know if I'll find jam or pickles in it."

However, loss of colour perception cannot be the cause of the recognition disorder, so we must conclude either that the cells affected are involved in both colour and form perception, or that the areas dealing with colour and form perception are anatomically close and are likely to be jointly affected by a lesion (see pp. 14–15). In this respect, it is interesting to note that some other agnosic patients are not achromatopsic. The patient of Benson and Greenberg (1969), for instance, had normal colour perception (see also Taylor & Warrington, 1971; Warrington & Shallice, 1984). This pattern, with some but not all agnosic patients having achromatopsia, suggests that form and colour processing simply take place in anatomically close areas of the brain—with the lesion affecting colour as well as form processing in some patients.

INABILITY TO FIND THE WAY—TOPOGRAPHICAL AGNOSIA

Patients with visual agnosia often have problems with finding their way around. This is easily understandable. The patient may no longer be able to recognise the objects that most of us use as cues signalling whether we should turn left or right (such as the pillar box on the corner). If the patient has lost their colour vision, they will be further handicapped; for example, we often use the colour of the door to distinguish a house from a row of similar ones.

Bornstein and Kidron's (1959) patient developed visual agnosia during the course of a journey by bus. His consequent difficulties have been very clearly documented:

The patient woke up with a severe frontal headache which lessened somewhat during the next three hours. He had an appointment at noon of the same day and caught a bus in order to go there, but on his way his headache increased, and he decided to go home instead. He alighted from his bus as he had to change his route and on his way to another bus stop, on a road well known to him, he felt all of a sudden that the whole area appeared strange. He knew where he was and could not account for it. He managed to cross the road—he knew he had to do that—and boarded the correct bus in order to reach home. He paid his fare and received a ticket. The route, obviously well known to him, appeared strange and for a time he thought he had caught the wrong bus. He became anxious, gave the driver his address and asked him to see that he reached home should anything happen to him meanwhile. When he thought that he had reached his stop he alighted, but not because he recognised the surroundings which appeared unfamiliar to him, but because he estimated that sufficient time had elapsed in order to arrive at it. He remembered these details clearly. He also remembered that while on the bus he found it difficult to distinguish men from women passengers. After getting off the bus, "I stood in the street and asked passers-by how to get to my home. I gave them my address and carried on in the direction indicated." After walking about five minutes, the approximate time needed to reach his home, he could not find it. He again turned to passers-by who told him to cross the road as the required number was on the opposite side of the street. "I eventually reached home, and though I knew it was my home, it seemed strange to me." He opened the door, entered the flat which he knew was his, but the room, the furniture and pictures appeared different.

A similar account is given by Pallis's (1955) patient: "At about eight o'clock the next morning I got out of bed. My mind was clear but I could not recognise the bedroom. I went to the toilet. I had difficulty in finding my way and recognising the place. Turning round to go back to bed I found I couldn't recognise the room, which was a strange place to me . . . ."

It might be suggested that the problem that these patients describe is simply due to memory loss. Due to the brain damage which occurred, they may have forgotten where they were and how they might make their way from A to B. However, Pallis's (1955) patient had a very good topographical memory. He could give accurate descriptions of paths, roads, and the layout of a mineshaft (he was previously a mining engineer). He also found no trouble in drawing maps of places familiar to him from before his illness. His problem was with reality; when he had to go from one place to another he was unable to recognise the places on the route. In order to find his way about he stated: "I have to keep the idea of the route in my head the whole time and count the turnings, as if I were following instructions that had been memorised."

It is possible to attribute the problems such patients encounter in finding their way to a primary disturbance in visual recognition. This may therefore occur in all varieties of visual agnosia. In other cases, though, the patients may have additional difficulty in calling up visual memories of objects and places. Clearly, this could supplement any recognition impairment and lead to further problems in direction finding.

PROBLEMS WITH VISUAL MEMORY

The agnosic patient described by Ratcliff and Newcombe (1982) produced painstakingly accurate copies of objects that he failed to recognise. When later asked to draw the object from memory, the patient typically gave very impoverished responses (see Fig. 5.1), though he could often give an appropriate verbal definition for the object. This discrepancy between accurate copying and rather poorer drawing from memory has also been observed in other patients with visual recognition deficits (e.g., Beyn & Knyazeva, 1962; Davidoff & Wilson, 1985). Possibly related to this, at least some agnosic patients later state that their dreams lack visual components. For instance, Adler (1950) noted that her patient "did not remember having seen anything in dreams since the beginning of her illness. She had heard people talk in her dreams . . .".

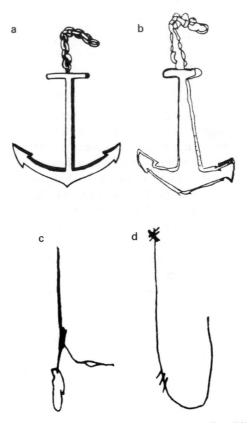

FIG. 5.1. Examples of copying and drawing from memory by Ratcliff and Newcombe's (1982) patient. a) model line drawing of an anchor; b) copy of line drawing; c) and d) attempts to draw the anchor from memory.

However, this lack of visual memory again only appears to be true of some patients, since others do retain their memory of the appearance of objects (e.g., Pallis, 1955; Wapner et al., 1978), and others have been shown to have a good retention of new visual material (Levine, 1978). Unfortunately, in many of the cases, visual memory ability has not been tested so we cannot be sure of the relation between memory deficits and the various types of agnosia. We can only conclude that poor visual memory is not the cause of all agnosias.

FAILURE TO RECOGNISE FAMILIAR FACES—PROSOPAGNOSIA

Possibly one of the most distressing aspects of visual agnosia is that patients may be unable to recognise faces, even the faces of those nearest and dearest to them. There seems to be very little that agnosic patients can use in the way of cues (e.g., particular head shape, jutting nose, bushy eyebrows etc.) to help them to recognise people. Pallis's (1955) patient stated that he had to wait for his wife or his mother to speak before he could distinguish between them. This was despite the fact that his mother was 80 years old and, presumably, would have had many more visible signs of age than his wife.

It is not as though patients with prosopagnosia cannot see the faces in front of them (just as the agnosic patient can "see" the object) it just seems that what they see does not add up sufficiently for them to know who it is. Macrae and Trolle's (1956) patient was very articulate in his account of his difficulties: "I can see the whole face—the bit I am looking at (pointing with his forefinger to a spot on the questioner's chin) is quite clear—I can see every hair quite clearly—but everything else is quite different, as though there was a thin layer all over it or as though it was out of focus. I feel that if only I could move something, everything would be clear—then I would have no difficulty." Pallis's (1955) patient had a similar story: "I can see eyes, nose and mouth quite clearly but they just don't add up. They all seem chalked in, like on a blackboard. I have to tell by the clothes or the voice whether it is a man or a woman, as the faces are all neutral, a dirty grey colour. The hair may help a lot or if there is a moustache. . . . All men appear unshaven."

Amongst the most bizarre aspects of the condition is that such patients are no longer able to recognise themselves. Earlier in this chapter an account was given of the difficulties experienced by Bornstein and Kidron's (1959) patient who developed visual agnosia during the course of a bus journey and who experienced great difficulty in finding his way home. When he eventually entered his flat, "The first thing I did was to go to the bathroom to wash. I looked in the mirror and saw a strange face. I put a cold compress on my forehead and, as far as I remember, lay down for about three hours".

While it is perhaps very understandable in the very early stages of the disorder for the patient not to recognise himself, as time passes it seems odd that some sort of familiarity does not develop, but this does not seem to occur. Macrae and Trolle's (1956) patient would frequently, especially when shaving, question whether the face staring at him from the mirror was really his own, and even though he knew it could be physically no other, on several occasions he found himself grimacing or sticking out his tongue "just to make sure".

As with other aspects of the recognition problem, the failure to recognise oneself can have embarrassing consequences. Pallis's (1955) patient recalls "At the club I saw someone strange staring at me and asked the steward who it was. You'll laugh at me. I'd been looking at myself in a mirror."

The failure to recognise familiar faces has disastrous implications for the everyday organisation of ones' life that can be helped a little by, for example, members of the family always sitting in the same place at mealtimes, or, when out of doors, wearing conspicuous articles of clothing as such as a large hat. Simple pleasures may, however, be forever marred. For instance, Pallis's (1955) patient ruefully states "I'd bought some copies of *Men Only* and *London Opinion*. I couldn't enjoy the usual pictures. I could work out what was what by accessory details but it is no fun that way. You've got to take it in at a glance."

Prosopagnosia may be the only recognition problem for some patients and because of this, it is often regarded as a separate disorder from visual object agnosia (e.g., Hécaen, 1981). However, it is not difficult to argue that faces, perhaps more than any other object, are extremely similar to each other. It is very important for us to be able to distinguish one face from another, we train ourselves to do it and many of us can proudly say "I never forget a face." However, this ability is often not so expert when we are faced with another race whose physiognomy is of a different colour or a different shape to that which we are accustomed to. Possibly faces are the most complex visual objects (in recognition terms) that people are typically able to individually identify—though we may acquire the ability to make similar distinctions between other highly similar exemplars within a given class, such as between cats from the same litter or different types of bird, if we particularly put our minds to the problem. Therefore, faces may be the only objects that a patient with a mild degree of visual object agnosia has difficulty in recognising (see Sergent, in press). Interestingly, there are a few cases where people with highly-developed skills in identifying animals demonstrate what might be termed "pure" prosopagnosia (i.e., a deficit in recognising faces but not common objects). In these patients the recognition problem extended from faces to animals (so that the patients could not distinguish, for instance, the cows in their herd; see Assal, Favre, & Anderes, 1984; Bornstein, Skroka, & Munitz, 1969). Similarly, Damasio, Damasio, and Van Hoesen (1982) write:

> In the three prosopagnosic patients . . . we investigated the success or failure of recognition of objects of daily usage by inquiring from both the patient and a close relative, on the subject's ability to recognise familiar automobiles, articles of clothing, cooking utensils and food ingredients. The notion that prosopagnosia is limited to agnosia for human faces proved easily falsifiable. All three had become unable to recognise and sort out their own cars and articles of clothing and all depended on their spouses to help them dress as intended. Patient 1, a woman, would confuse foodstuffs and required help in her cooking. To select articles from the shelves of the supermarket, she had to read every label, whereas before, the mere shape and size of containers would permit the correct choice. Patients 2 and 3 depended on their wives to find their cars, whereas patient 1 developed an expert way of dealing with the problem. She memorised the license plate of the vehicle, and, in order to find it in parking lots, she would systematically scan the number of every car plate until she found that of her car. The appearance of the car itself was of no assistance to her.

From this discussion, it seems likely that problems in face recognition will often be part of a general recognition disorder. This is not to state that all problems in face or object recognition will be for the same reason. What is needed is to distinguish more accurately between the types of agnosic patient, and indeed, between what are probably different types of prosopagnosia. Here we would expect that disorders due to a loss of stored knowledge about stimuli could be specific to different classes of object; that is, one might lose knowledge about faces but not objects, or vice versa. In contrast, the problems in organising visual input appropriately that seem to occur for John should produce a common impairment to object and face recognition that, in its least severe form, will only affect faces.

DIFFICULTIES IN READING—ALEXIA

Most people are now aware that some children find learning to read extremely difficult, even though they appear to have a normal intellect in other ways. This specific problem in reading is termed "dyslexia" (meaning disruption in the processes of word recognition and reading). Following brain damage, adults who were previously able to read fluently may find their reading impaired. When this impairment is sufficient to effectively eliminate the normal reading process, the disorder is termed "alexia" (meaning the complete loss of the processes of word recognition and reading). Some cases of agnosia have suffered this complete loss of the ability to read. For instance, the patients documented by Benson and Greenberg (1969) and Campion (in press) were unable to identify single letters successfully. The same was also true initially of Adler's patient (Adler, 1944). The problem encountered by these patients does not entail the loss of letter names or sounds; rather, it seemed to relate to their general problem in analysing visual input. For instance, Adler's patient was able only to pick up parts of a letter at a time. Thus she named a *K* as a "capital I", and, when asked to draw what she had seen, drew the single line of the I. Later she learned to guess identities from the partial information she perceived. She learned to identify numbers first, presumably because there are fewer possibilities and because they are often composed of simple straight lines. She stated that "In a 6 there is only a lower loop. If I find an upper loop too, I know it is a 3. If there is only an upper loop, it is a 9. There are two circles in the 8." It is apparent that the patient is using the same feature-by-feature strategy here as she used to identify objects (see p. 18). Eight years after the lesion occurred, she had progressed to reading books—though *A Tree Grows in Brooklyn* took three months to complete due to her protracted letter recognition. Interestingly, she remained unable to read unfamiliar words because she could not use her prior knowledge when attempting to recognise them. Much of the improvement observed in this patient appears to be due to her ability to make informed guesses from very impaired perceptual processes. In other patients, the reading problem is less severe. For example, the patients described by Rubens and Benson (1971) and by Wapner et al. (1978) were generally able to identify single letters, but were only able to read words slowly by spelling them aloud letter-by-letter. Other processes, such as the patients' knowledge about the word and its spelling appeared intact. Rubens and Benson (1971) write: "In contrast to the slow, tedious process of reading, he rapidly comprehended words that were spelled aloud and words written in the palm of either hand. Similarly, he could spell out loud without difficulty."

Unless patients remark that they have to read letter-by-letter, or unless they are only able to do this by reading each letter aloud (rather than by saying it to themselves), this deficit may go unnoticed, since the patients may identify the words correctly. In many case studies it is only commented that the patients can identify words correctly. The time it takes them to do so, and whether this time increases dramatically as a function of word length, is not generally noted. Unfortunately, this also means that we have no clear idea of the processes the patients have to go through to reach their final correct response. From the above analysis, it seems that patients who appear to have problems in some of the "early" processes in visual recognition, such as incorrectly registering and organising form elements, also encounter problems in word recognition. This seems to be a common deficit. However, once again we should be cautious in generalising this conclusion to all agnosic patients. If patients selectively lose their stored knowledge about the functions of objects or their prior associations with them, this need not necessarily affect the ability to name words. After all, we are able to read aloud words without knowing their precise meaning. Thus we might expect at least some patients to name words with surprising facility even when they appear to have lost stored knowledge about objects, and so do not know what the words mean. This appears to be true of some patients with generalised cerebral atrophy (e.g., Shallice & Warrington, 1980; Shallice, Warrington, & McCarthy, 1983).

JOHN'S ADDITIONAL VISUAL PROCESSING PROBLEMS

We have suggested that John has a selective problem in "binding" individual form elements together. Nevertheless, he has global shape information available. This suggests that the global shape processing, and the coding of relations between form elements, are separate processes in vision.

What are the effects of John's visual processing impairment on other component processes in vision? If his problem is indeed selective, it is possible that many other visual functions are intact. This would give us a privileged view of what comprise distinct processing modules in vision.

Depth and Movement

In one of our first assessments of John's problem, we gave him examples of many standard visual illusions, such as the Müller-Lyer and Ponzo (see Figs. 3.5 and 3.6). He appeared to be susceptible to the illusions. If we attribute these illusions to the implicit use of the local depth cues offered by the perspective in the drawings (e.g., Gregory, 1970; see Chapter 3, Fig. 3.5), this finding suggests that John is sensitive to these depth cues. Perhaps the individual line elements do not need to have their relative positions accurately coded for such cues to arise, or perhaps it does not matter if the relative positions of the lines are coded in a slow and effortful fashion. Whatever the case, it appears that John cannot ignore the surrounding context when judging the length of the relevant lines. Thus, though he might be poor at "binding" features together, he seems obliged to engage in this process. This confirms our earlier impression from the "real object–new object" and the "global–local" letter identification tasks

(Figs. 4.8 and 4.10), where the presence of extra local features impaired his performance.

The local depth cues in the Müller-Lyer and Ponzo illusions are due to perspective. We also queried whether he was sensitive to depth from binocular disparities. He was given sets of random dot stereograms, containing varying degrees of disparity information (Julesz, 1971). He showed a good ability to achieve stereo depth, describing the stereo figures as standing out in 3D.

However, although John is capable of resolving local monocular cues to depth (as in the Müller-Lyer and Ponzo illusions), and of seeing depth stereoscopically (with random dot stereograms), we should not assume that his depth perception is absolutely normal. Normal depth perception is probably based on integrated descriptions of the local parts of objects— including accurate coding of shading and the "texture" of the surface of different objects (since objects which are closer will tend to have "expanded" textures). The coding of the surfaces of the objects may then be embellished by the addition of stereoscopic depth information (Chapter 3, p. 55). Now, because of his problem in grouping form information, John is very bad at dealing with shadows—he typically uses shadows to segment a surface into two or more "parts", instead of coding the information as constituting a single surface at different depths. This suggests that his representation of an object will often fail to "mesh" with the depth cues provided stereoscopically, since single surfaces are segmented into unconnected parts. Consequently, although some of the components of depth perception seem intact (such as stereoscopic vision), he may not be able to use the information appropriately. It may be for this reason that he now experiences discomfort when being driven, since cars appear too close and appear to "loom" towards him (Chapters 2 and 7).

John also comments that he finds it easier to identify moving rather than stationary objects. This is most apparent with animals, which he finds extremely difficult to identify when stationary (or photographed), and considerably easier when they move and generate a characteristic movement pattern. John also tried to rely on his wife's gait when attempting to identify her. His detection of movement and motion patterns has not yet been tested formally, though there appears to be no obvious deficit. He can grasp moving objects appropriately, he can catch a ball etc. While our final conclusions on this matter await detailed research, it does seem that his motion perception is also (at least relatively) normal. Thus his case backs up the proposition that visual processing contains separate modules for depth, motion and static form perception. To this we can now add that there are separate modules for coding the locations of form elements and for combining the form elements into perceptual wholes.

Colour

In contrast to his apparently normal depth and motion perception, John's colour perception is drastically impaired. He reports that the world is now composed of objects of various shades of grey, and his colour discrimination is extremely poor. He fails at all the standard tests of colour vision, despite the fact that prior to the stroke, his colour vision was normal. Although this cannot be thought to be the primary cause of his recognition deficit, it is undoubtedly a contributory factor. In everyday life it adds to his difficulty in discriminating various items of clothing, between flowers and weeds etc. As we have already noted, there is a close link between lesions of the type and location suffered by John and both colour and form perception deficits (Meadows, 1974—see pp. 14–15). This may be either because the lesion implicates separate colour and form processing areas, or because colour and form information are integrally involved in visual perception (e.g., the cells may code both colour and form).

At present, we favour the first position, because there is not a perfect relationship between cerebral achromatopsia and integrative agnosia (p. 84), and because, in normal vision, subjects can sometimes attend to just the colour of an object whilst ignorning its form and vice versa (e.g., Hillyard & Munte, 1984; Humphreys, 1981). If colour and form were integrally involved in visual perception, we would not just be able to attend selectively to either the colour or the form of a stimulus. One further point about John's colour processing is also worthy of mention. This is that, on occasion, his memory of the colour of objects is unreliable. This problem was uncovered in tests where we gave him the name of an object, and then asked him a series of questions to test his knowledge. On the vast majority of these questions, he performed at a high standard, and he had no apparent difficulty in reporting characteristics such as the size or weight of objects, which one would imagine required stored visual knowledge. In this respect, his answers were consistent with his good drawing from memory (pp. 65–67): he appears to have intact knowledge about object form. However, when questioned about the colour of objects his responses were sometimes surprising; for instance, he said that an elephant would be green, and that a polar bear would be grey. Although this problem was not very pronounced, the contrast with his knowledge of object form invites the argument that his colour memory is damaged. One intriguing possibility is that the brain mechanisms supporting colour perception are the same as those which support colour memory—with the colour perceptual system perhaps being "reactivated" when we remember the colour of an object. However, memory for object form seems to be independent of those parts of the perceptual system concerned with the early processing of form, since only the latter is markedly impaired in John.

TS–G

Visual Memory

John's drawings from memory suggest that his stored visual knowledge about objects is essentially intact. The only objects he remarks on as being difficult to draw from memory are flowers. We concur with his conclusion. Although one of his main hobbies before his stroke was gardening, and he remains able to quote the Latin names of plants, he finds it difficult to differentiate between different types of plants when he draws them from memory. Such drawings tend to take on a generic flower shape, and they fail to preserve the characteristics of individual flowers (see Fig. 5.2). It is certainly possible that this does represent some residual impairment in John's stored visual memory; though, even if this were true, it could not explain his object recognition problem, since he can draw almost all the other objects that he has difficulty in identifying. Alternatively, it could be that flowers are a particularly difficult kind of object to draw from memory (at least for an unskilled artist), and his difficulty in drawing them, though real, is nothing out of the ordinary.

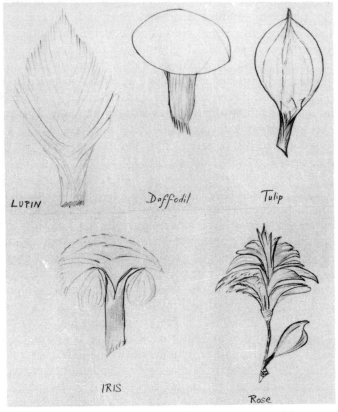

FIG. 5.2.   Examples of John's drawings from memory of flowers.

In addition to having a generally intact long-term memory, John also seems to have a good ability to retain new visual information. For instance, he notices if we re-present line drawings to him during a testing session, even though he may be unable to identify the object on both occasions. In more formal tests, we presented pairs of letters to him, one letter at a time, and he had to decide if the pair had the same name (i.e., respond "yes" to *AA* and *Aa*; respond "no" to *AB*). When control subjects perform this task, they are faster to match *AA* than *Aa*, providing the interval between the letters is no longer than about 1.5 seconds. This shows that they hold the "form" of the letter in memory for about that duration, so that match times are quicker when the "form" as well as the name of the letters is the same (i.e., if both letters are upper case, responses are faster than if one is upper and the other lower case; see Posner, 1969). When given this test, John demonstrated a normal pattern of performance. His short-term visual memory is not impaired. There thus appears to be a functional distinction between memorial and perceptual processes in form recognition, with John having only impaired perceptual processes.

Finding his Way

Along with his inability to recognise objects, faces and colours, John's main complaint concerns his problem in finding his way. This problem is apparent both when he has to re-trace once well-known routes (such as around his old house), and when he has to learn new routes (such as from his new flat to the shops). The problem seems to be so gross, and so time-consuming to those trying to help him learn a route, that one might imagine that his "route memory" is somehow impaired. Perhaps our memory for routes is quite distinct from other types of long-term memory, so that it can be selectively impaired. To test this possibility, we asked John to draw various maps from memory. In Fig. 5.3 we show his map of the route from his flat to the local shops, alongside that drawn by his wife, Iris. John's map is accurate, although the distances are perhaps a little distorted—yet it is still quite a common occurrence for him to lose his way on this route, especially if he is distracted by meeting people along the way. His problem in losing his way is not due to a particular defect in his "route memory".

With regards to John's route-finding difficulty, it is interesting to note his verbal description of the route from his house to the shops, which he described as being 240 paces away (Chapter 2). This suggests that visual cues do not play a large part in his navigating the route; rather the route is coded in terms of the number of walking paces in particular directions. Normally, we may use visual cues to help us learn a route, and to help us navigate it. Indeed, there are many less-familiar routes we may travel using

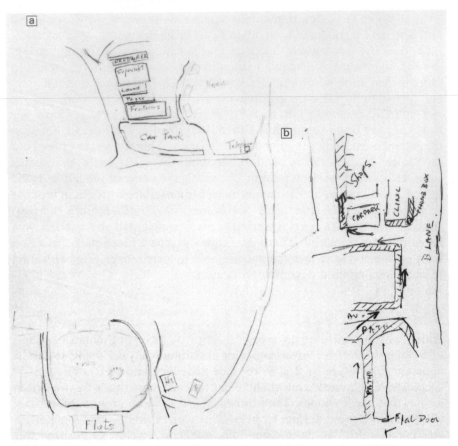

FIG. 5.3.   The route from the new flat to the shops: a) John's version; b) Iris's version.

only visual landmarks to tell us the next direction to take—when we don't have a good overall "mental picture" of the way. This is certainly the experience of one of the authors when travelling to some of the hospitals where we occasionally test patients! John is impaired at using these landmarks, especially as many of the landmarks we may use (such as particular buildings or trees) are precisely the kinds of objects he finds difficult to differentiate, presumably because it is only detailed information about the "parts" that separates one building or one tree from another. Because he cannot use the landmarks, John is poor at finding his way. He is also slow to learn new routes, as he requires a lot of practice to translate a route into the kind of overall mental picture that we have with very familiar routes, where we might not need to be guided by visual landmarks. Further, if John is interrupted whilst making his way, so that he momentarily "forgets" his mental picture, he will often not know his whereabouts since he cannot use visual landmarks to re-orient himself. His task becomes rather like trying to find one's way in heavy jungle without a map, where it is extremely difficult to use visual cues to guide one back to the correct route.[1]

Reading

When we first saw John, he was able to read single letters correctly, but he was slow to read complete words. Although he did not name each letter aloud, he appeared to be reading "letter-by-letter" because his naming times increased directly in relation to the length of the words. Three-letter words took about three seconds to name, five-letter words about six seconds, and seven-letter words about ten seconds. His reading was also strongly affected by the visual characteristics of the script. Headlines in block capitals tended to be easier than passages in lower-case, and handwriting was practically impossible to read. In contrast, his own ability to write was relatively spared, the only problem being occasional letter substitutions, which seemed to reflect the visual similarity of the letters (with b–p substitutions being most common). The fact that his reading was so strongly affected by the visual characteristics of the script suggests that it is the visual processes in reading that prove difficult. John has not lost knowledge about word meanings, nor about how they are spelt; rather he seems poor at deriving the appropriate visual information to allow word recognition to proceed normally. Handwriting proves to be especially difficult because it requires appropriate coding and grouping of the strokes. An example of one of John's errors illustrates this. When we set him the task of drawing objects from memory (pp. 65–67), we wrote the names of the objects at the top of blank sheets of paper. When we received the completed forms we were quite surprised to find the drawing shown in Fig. 5.4 in place of what we had hoped to be a drawing of a mouse! However, John had failed to "group" the two loops of the handwritten "m", and so read the word as "house". This kind of grouping process probably needs to be conducted simultaneously across handwritten words for them to be read normally, since the coding of one letter may often be contingent on the coding of other letters in the word.

One might think that even if reading is slow it should not be too debilitating providing it is accurate. Thus John should be able to comprehend the passages he reads, though it may take him a long time to read them. Unfortunately, this is not true. We asked him to read aloud some passages to us. The word identification process itself was so slow that it was difficult for anyone to pick up the sense of the passage, to link the

---

[1]This analogy was suggested by Hilary Lawson.

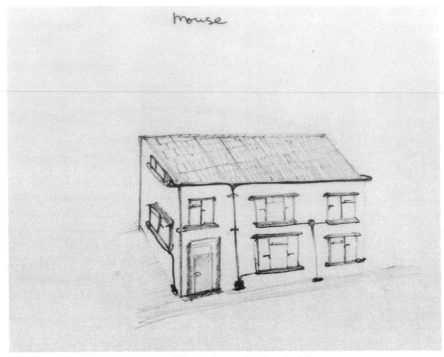

FIG. 5.4.   An example of John's difficulty in reading handwriting.

sentences together. Some idea of this may be picked up by reading the following passage:

xwxxhxxexxnx xyxxoxxux xtxxrxxyx xtxxox xrxxexxaxxdxx xwxxoxxrxxdxxsx xcxxoxxnxxsxxtxxrxxuxxcxxtxxexxdx xfxxrxxoxxmx xlxxexxtxxtxxexxrxxsx xwxxhxxixxcxxhx   xaxxrxxex   xsxxexxpxxaxxrxxaxxtxxexxdx   xixxnx xtxxhxxixxsx xsxxtxxrxxaxxnxxgxxex xwxxaxxyx xixxtx xixxsx xax xsxxuxxrxxpxxrxxixxsxxixxnxxgxxlxxyx   xsxxlxxoxxwx, xdxxixxfxxfxxixxcxxuxxlxxtx xbxxuxxsxxixxnxxexxsxxsx, xaxxnxxdx xixxtx xrxxexxqxxuxxixxrxxexxsx xsxxuxxcxxhx xaxxnx xexxfxxfxxoxxrxxtx xoxxfx xcxxoxxnxxcxxexxnxxtxxrxxaxxtxxixxoxxnx   xtxxhxxaxxtx   xyxxoxxux xtxxexxnxxdx   xtxxox   xfxxoxxrxxgxxexxtx   xtxxhxxex xmxxexxaxxnxxixxnxxgx xoxxfx xwxxhxxaxxtx xhxxaxxsx xgxxoxxxnxxex xbxxexxfxxoxxrxxex.

Studies of reading have shown that our comprehension of texts can be helped by keeping a kind of running memory record of the words in the sentence (e.g., Baddeley, 1979). This memory record may only last for a short time period unless we "refresh" it by saying the word over to ourselves (e.g., Schweickert & Boruff, 1986). John is prevented from doing this because of the effort involved in reading each word. Consequently, his comprehension may be impaired because his slow reading means that the record of each word decays before it can be linked to the other words in the sentence.

One of our colleagues, Susan Rickard, gave John a set of training procedures to help his reading. Each week he was given a short passage taken from his usual newspaper. He was asked to read it aloud and to keep a time of how long each reading took. The idea behind this procedure was quite straightforward. After reading the same passage a few times, the patient should be able to remember the general gist, if not some of the precise wording. The work load involved in comprehending the passage should therefore be much reduced, and the patient should practise the visual processes involved in reading each word. Also, as the passage becomes more familiar, the patient should start to use more predictive strategies and to sample the visual information on the page more efficiently.

Using these procedures in the first few months after his stroke, John did show some small improvements. Since then he has continued to practise reading, and tackles his favourite daily newspaper every day. Recently, along with another colleague, Cathy Price, we have returned to test his reading more thoroughly. These tests showed that his rates for reading single words have improved considerably since he was first tested. He now names three-letter words in about two-and-a-half seconds, five-letter words in about three seconds and seven-letter words in about four-and-a-half seconds. His perseverance here does appear to have paid dividends. One interesting aspect of his improvement is that his rates for naming words which occur frequently in the language are now about twice as fast as those for low-frequency words; formerly naming times to high-frequency words were only slightly faster than to low-frequency words. This suggests that his increased reading speeds may not reflect increased uptake of visual information; rather he seems better able to interpret that information in terms of a set of high-frequency words that he encounters fairly regularly.

A SUMMARY

Like most agnosic patients, John also has an array of ancillary problems. He has no colour vision, he has great difficulties recognising faces and finding his way, and, though his reading is accurate, it is slow and effortful. He does not have any problems with visual memory, however.

John's lack of colour vision is not the cause of his recognition problems, and it may be most easily attributed to the anatomical proximity of the brain areas concerned with colour and with form perception. The lesion suffered by John seems to have involved both areas. One interesting aspect of this is that his long-term memory for the colour of objects also appears to have some minor impairments. It may be that colour perception and colour memory draw on the same brain areas. On the other hand, form perception and memory do not appear to do so, since John's form memory is a good deal better than his form perception.

The other ancillary problems, concerning route finding, face recognition, and reading, all seem to be due to his basic recognition impairment. Because the recognition impairment reflects damage to quite an "early" component of the processing chain, perceptual organisation, it will influence all behaviours requiring visual input to be organised efficiently—whether the original stimulus is an object, landmarks along a route, a face or a word. Of course, it remains possible that patients with some kind of "higher-order" problem (such as the loss of particular types of memory) may have only some of these ancillary problems (e.g., they may name words normally but not objects). Our conclusions about the relations between agnosia and its associated deficits must take into account the type of agnosia involved.

One point that does emerge from John's descriptions of his problems in finding his way is that he may often make what appear to be "silly" errors because the whole process is so effortful. Now, when we are engaged in any effortful mental process—such as trying to work out a particularly difficult problem—we make errors because we fail to concentrate on other aspects of our behaviour. For instance, we may find ourselves driving along a familiar route instead of turning off earlier because we were "thinking of something else at the time". Imagine then the extra problems of this sort that may occur when all our recognition processes have become slow and effortful, as they have for John. It seems little wonder that such patients will sometimes appear to have "lapses of concentration", which exacerbate the recognition problems. This aspect of John's behaviour is taken up in Chapter 7.

6 Some Conclusions About Agnosia and Visual Recognition

JOHN'S VISUAL RECOGNITION

John has the rare complaint of visual agnosia, and, even amongst the agnosic population, he is a rare patient because his deficits are so selective. He has no memory or intellectual impairment, and he remains a very articulate, intelligent man.

In our study we have tried to slot the pieces of the jigsaw, his case, into some semblance of order. Our initial hunch about the form of the jigsaw, is provided by the account of the processes normally involved in visual recognition, which we gave in Chapter 3. We suggested that visual recognition is the result of a number of processes, each of which may, to some extent, operate independently (see also Humphreys & Riddoch, in press/a; Riddoch & Humphreys, in press/b). For instance, the recognition of static forms may require the following operations:

1. The correct registration of the constituents of form perception, line and edge elements at their correct positions and orientations, and at different spatial scales (i.e., including both "fine" and "coarse" elements—see pp. 54–55);
2. the correct "binding together" of these form elements to generate perceptual wholes, and to allow the "figure" to be separated from the "ground" (p. 55);
3. the assignment of orientation to the whole object, so that it can be recognised from different viewpoints (p. 56);

4. the memory of the object's shape, to match against the representation of the object derived from process 3 above;
5. the memory of the object's function and one's prior associations with it; and
6. the processes that match what we might term the representations derived from the input (points 1–3) with the memories denoted by points 4 and 5.

To these processes we might also add processes concerned with assigning depth and movement to the form information, processes that link up the "local" depth assignments to form a "global" interpretation of the object or scene (see Figs. 3.9 and 3.10), and processes which use our stored knowledge about objects to influence operations occurring earlier on in the processing chain (pp. 44–49).

We have argued that John suffers a specific problem in "binding together" the local parts of objects simultaneously at different spatial locations (process 2, pp. 72–79). Our initial diagnosis was based on both positive and negative evidence: the positive being his feature-by-feature copying and identification strategies; the negative being the fact that he is able to copy and that he has good long-term memory for the appearance and functions of the objects he fails to recognise. This negative evidence rules out the possibility that his problem occurs either because of faulty processing of local form features, or because of an impaired memory of either the shape or the functions of objects (points 1, 4, and 5, pp. 68–72). Because of his problem in combining form elements, John is often unable to organise the parts of objects correctly to embellish global information about the whole object. This means that he often fails to group two parts that belong to the same object, that he segments the parts as belonging to different objects, and, therefore, that he fails to code what is figure and what is ground correctly. These problems are exemplified by his identification errors—where, for instance, he segments a paintbrush into two objects (p. 60).

We have also tried to go beyond this initial diagnosis to consider some of the processes of perceptual organisation which are disrupted in John's case. For instance, he appears to have relatively normal stereoscopic depth and movement perception, consistent with the existence of separate processing modules for the perception of stereoscopic depth, movement, and static form.

Studies of his "visual search" (pp. 74–77) assessed in more detail his form perception. These studies confirmed that John has a selective problem in "binding" form elements together simultaneously, though his ability to detect single-line targets and to conduct difficult item-by-item searches (in circumstances where control subjects also search item by item) was shown to be intact. These studies also showed that he could derive "global" information about the overall shape of objects but, unlike normal subjects, his global descriptions of objects are not elaborated by detailed coding of the "parts". We may conclude from this that such global shape descriptions can be derived independently of the processes involved in "binding" the local parts together. This conclusion is consistent with workers in the field of computer vision, who have argued that form perception first involves filtering input at different spatial scales—from coarse to fine. The filtered information is then combined in a second, separate operation. John seems selectively impaired at this second "feature-binding" process, which he can only conduct upon one group of features at a time. One result of this is that his "coarse" information about objects is separated from the "fine" details.

Interestingly, once John has coded the relations within a group of local features, he is able to link this coding with other local interpretations from different spatial regions to form a global interpretation of the scene (pp. 79–80). Thus, he can identify some of the ambiguities in the Hogarth etching (Fig. 3.9), though his detailed coding of the relations between the lines in each region is faulty, and only operates in a slow and effortful manner. It appears then that we can separate two "linking operations" in perception. One concerns coding the relations between lines within a spatial region—which may normally happen within a single glance at a scene. This is impaired in John. The other concerns coding the relations across spatial regions—which seems to be relatively intact in John. We may speculate that this second "linking" process involves building a kind of "working memory" of a scene—perhaps by integrating information across eye movements (e.g., Hochberg, 1968, 1978). If so, John's ability to carry out this "linking" process would accord with his having an intact eye-movement system.

John is also able to take advantage of contextual cues to help him identify objects, so that he is generally much better at identifying objects seen in their appropriate context than he is at identifying them in isolation (p. 80). However, this improvement seems to occur primarily because the context suggests the hypotheses that he uses to match against his impaired perceptual information. Unlike normal subjects, he seems unable to use context to organise his perceptions—he is unable to suddenly "see" an object where before there existed only unorganised visual information (as we sometimes experience when viewing ambiguous figures). On this topic, our experimental studies simply confirm what one might conclude from his general behaviour. If John could use context to "see" objects as detailed perceptual wholes, he should be able to do this when looking at, say, his own or his wife's face; this, of course, he is unable to do (see Chapter 2.) John's inability to use contextual information normally is also relevant to our ideas about what constitutes "normal" visual recognition. In general terms, his case supports the view that "perceptual" and "recognition" processes are separable, because his stored knowledge required for recognition is intact. The notion we discussed in Chapter 4 (p. 56), that recognition consists of matching perceptual information against stored memories seems appropriate here. John's case supports the view that the perceptual representation used in this matching process can be "driven" solely by stimulus information, so that it is unaffected by contextual knowledge. This means that the input is "organised" using general principles which apply across all types of objects—and that the principles are not confined to particular objects in particular contexts. This suggestion follows the line originated by the Gestalt psychologists (Chapter 3, p. 44). Nevertheless, contextual knowledge may normally guide perceptual organisation on some occasions—particularly when the stimulus information is ambiguous. John's perception seems immune from such guidance.

TYPES OF AGNOSIA (REVISITED)

In Chapter 1 we discussed Lissauer's long-standing proposition that there exist two distinct types of agnosic patient. Apperceptive agnosics are thought to have difficulty in perceptual processing; associative agnosics are thought to have intact perceptual processing, but have difficulty linking the products of this perceptual processing with their stored memories about objects.

Considered in terms of Lissauer's distinction, John is something of a puzzle. He performs well on copying tests, which are usually taken to indicate intact perceptual processes in clinical settings, and yet there are good grounds for arguing that his perceptual processes are far from normal (Chapter 4). This indicates that accurate copying should not be taken as diagnostic of normal perceptual processes. At the very least, some note of the copying strategy should be taken, since a slavish line-by line strategy might indicate poor perceptual integration of form features. Even better would be to conduct more rigorous tests of early visual processing.

A second point is that John seems different from other "apperceptive" agnosic patients who seem impaired at discriminating between shapes (e.g., Adler, 1944, 1950; Benson & Greenberg, 1969; Campion, in press; Campion & Latto, 1985—see pp. 16–18), because John shows good discrimination of local form features. This suggests that patients may have different types of perceptual impairment, so that the general term "apperceptive agnosia" fails to distinguish between them. Indeed, if we take the view that visual recognition involves more than the two processes of apperception and association proposed by Lissauer, as we have suggested in Chapter 4, then it seems possible that selective disturbance to these multiple processes could precipitate a number of different types of what might be more generally termed "apperceptive" or "associative" agnosia. That is, we may need to separate both the apperception and the association processes into their component operations, to give a more accurate account of the different patients who reflect selective damage to these different operations. The following sections distinguish between five different sub-classes of patient who have been previously described in the literature (see Humphreys & Riddoch, in press/b for a detailed discussion).

Shape Agnosia

This classification refers to patients whose initial registration of the elements of form perception seems impaired. Such patients should be unable to copy the stimuli they cannot recognise, and they may show poor discrimination between shapes. Thus some of the patients often thought of as classic instances of apperceptive agnosia may fall into this category (e.g., Adler, 1944; 1950; Benson & Greenberg, 1969; Campion, in press; Campion & Latto, 1985). As we noted in Chapter 1, the patients documented so far who may be thought of in this way all appear to have suffered from carbon monoxide poisoning. Carbon monoxide can have the effect of producing a peppering of small lesions in the cortex, almost as if the cortex had been hit by lead shot (Plum, Posner, & Hain, 1962; Richardson, Chambers, & Heywood, 1959). From this, Campion (Campion, in press; Campion & Latto, 1985) has speculated that there may be many small areas of decreased sensitivity or even blindness in the patient's visual fields, impairing the registration of forms which fall across these areas. To such patients, the world may be composed of fragments of contours.

Integrative Agnosia

This term may be applied to patients such as John, who appear to have intact registration of form elements, along with an impaired ability to integrate the elements into perceptual wholes. Such patients may be able to copy the objects they fail to recognise, but their copying procedures ought not to be normal. They ought also to identify objects using feature-by-feature descriptions. As we noted in Chapter 1, feature-by-feature identification strategies can occur both with patients who can and cannot copy the objects that they misidentify, and it is therefore, not in itself diagnostic of integrative agnosia. Still, we would not expect (and indeed do not find) this strategy in patients who do appear to have intact perceptual representations of objects.

Patients who may be classed as integrative agnosics usually appear to have suffered some sort of vascular disturbance (such as a stroke) producing bilateral damage in the posterior regions of the brain (e.g., Albert et al., 1975; Mack & Boller, 1977; Wapner et al., 1978).

Transformation Agnosia

Patients that we have termed "shape" and "integrative" agnosics seem to have problems in generating normal perceptual representations of objects. Other patients have been described who have problems in visual recognition, but who do seem to have an intact perceptual representation. For instance, some patients have a problem in identifying objects seen from an unusual angle, though they may not otherwise experience recognition difficulties. Clearly, this type of recognition problem is not nearly so incapacitating as other forms of agnosia. It appears to occur because the patients find it difficult to compensate for the fact that the image of an object on the retina is transformed and changed as the object is rotated (particularly when the object is rotated in depth). Consequently, their recognition tends to be viewpoint-dependent, leading to problems with objects in unusual views (Humphreys & Riddoch, 1984; and see p. 56, Chapter 4). Such patients have been described both by ourselves (Humphreys & Riddoch, 1984; Riddoch & Humphreys, 1986) and by Professor Warrington of the National Hospital, London (Warrington, 1982; 1985; Warrington & Taylor, 1973; 1978). This problem in recognising transformed objects tends to be associated with damage to the parietal lobe, particularly of the right hemisphere.

Semantic Agnosia

So far, we have considered the kinds of problems in visual recognition that may occur due to an impairment to operations up to the matching of input information with stored knowledge of objects. However, it is also possible that a disturbance in object recognition could occur if there is disruption to the patient's stored knowledge of objects. If we draw on the framework for visual recognition offered in Chapter 3, it is clear that it will do a patient no good to have completely intact perceptual processing and grouping if there is no stored knowledge to match against any perceptual representations.

There are some cases of visual recognition disturbance which can be attributed most easily to the patient having disrupted stored knowledge about objects. If there is disruption to the patient's (semantic) knowledge about the meaning and functions of objects, the problem may be classed as semantic agnosia. In some cases the loss of meaning may not be specific to vision, but will apply also when the patient feels the object or hears its name. A patient fitting this description was reported by Taylor and Warrington (1971). This patient had marked problems in recognising common objects by sight. However, he additionally had problems in recognising objects from touch, so that the patient "attempted to cut paper with a screwdriver rather than the scissors placed in front of him" and "on an occasion when it was raining he was taken outside and given a closed umbrella. He did not know how to use it and only when it was held over him did he appear to recognise it". He also had a problem in understanding what was said to him. For example, when asked "How is your wife?" he replied, "What does 'wife' mean?" Nevertheless, the patient was able to copy objects and he could judge whether objects were the same when seen in different views (even though he did not know what they were). These general problems concerned with knowing the meaning of objects whether seen, heard or touched can be attributed to the loss of semantic knowledge. Unlike the patient we have discussed hitherto, Taylor and Warrington's patient was suffering from a generalised cerebral atrophy, and the loss of semantic knowledge may be characteristic in severe cases of this type (see Marin, in press). More recently, Warrington and Shallice (1984) have documented similar problems in patients who had contracted the virus herpes simplex encephalitis. Contraction of this virus is associated with diffuse damage to the temporal lobes in both cerebral hemispheres. Rather than cerebral atrophy per se, then, it may be that damage to the temporal lobes precipitates the loss of semantic knowledge, with this damage also occurring in cases of widespread cerebral atrophy. This would fit in with the suggestion that the temporal lobe is implicated at the "end" of the processing chain in visual recognition (see Fig. 1.3 p. 15).

Semantic Access Agnosia

It is also possible that patients may exist with both intact perceptual processing and intact knowledge about objects, but whose problem is in matching the products of perception with their knowledge. Such patients would match Lissauer's (1890) theoretical account of associative agnosia. We choose to term the patients "semantic access agnosics" because the new term does not carry the connotation that this is one of just the two types of agnosia which occur (the other being apperceptive agnosia).

Recently, we have documented a patient whom we believe fits into this category (Riddoch & Humphreys, in press/c). This patient had been in a road traffic accident which had resulted in damage to the temporal and parietal lobes on the left side of the brain. After the accident he was often unable to recognise objects from vision. For instance, he was poor at judging whether two objects (such as a hammer and a nail) would be used together. The problem was specific to vision since he could do this task easily if he was told the objects' names. Also, unlike integrative and shape agnosics, the patient was good at judging whether he had seen an object before or whether it was one that we had constructed (see Fig. 4.8, p. 73). Typically, he stated that "objects were familiar", but that he could not remember what they were or what he could do with them. This suggests that when he looked at an object, he knew that its shape was familiar, but that his problem lay in associating that shape with its function. Given that the patient could discriminate familiar objects from unfamiliar objects, his recognition impairment could not be attributed to an impoverished perceptual representation of form. Also, his identification errors did not consist of the feature-by-feature descriptions of integrative and shape agnosics; rather they comprised prompt namings of objects that were both from the same general class and that also resembled the target object.

A SUMMARY

John's case allows us to make some conclusions both about how visual recognition normally occurs, and about the relations between different recognition disorders (types of agnosia). His selective impairment at "binding" local features together suggests that this is a distinct process in visual recognition, and separate from other processing modules concerned with the registration of form information and with coding stereoscopic depth and movement. These perceptual processes also seem to be distinct from our stored memories of the shape of different objects. It appears that the "binding" of local form features needs to take place simultaneously at different spatial regions to enable groupings, and later recognition, to operate normally.

John's selective disability further indicates that we need to distinguish between a range of recognition disorders, and that the two-stage account offered by Lissauer (1890) will no longer suffice. It seems likely that many varieties of agnosia exist. If in future we are to help such patients, we need diagnostic tools which specify the particular problems the patient encounters. Perhaps case studies such as the present one will help to refine future diagnoses.

The final word, however, should go to John and Iris, who have had to cope with John's recognition problems, and his changed visual world, on a day-to-day basis. The lessons they have learned in doing this, and their resolution to live as normal a life as possible, are lessons for us all.

7 Living With Visual Agnosia

After five years of testing, we think we now know something about the "why" of visual agnosia—at least as far as integrative visual agnosia is concerned. The information we have gathered, and are continuing to gather, has been of great benefit in supporting certain theories of normal visual processing. But what of John? He has had to live with the disorder for five years and has had to learn to come to terms with it. It has greatly affected his life. He has had to take premature retirement. How does he manage to live from day to day in his greatly altered and confusing visual world? The answer is given in the words of Iris:

"We both have to be very methodical in the house and remember to put things back in exactly the same place every day. In spite of this he would often find himself cleaning his teeth with his shaving cream or trying to put my blouse on instead of his shirt.

One of my biggest problems was how to keep him from boredom. We had always done crossword puzzles together by me reading out the clues and both of us supplying the answers. I soon found that this was excellent therapy as his long-term memory was good and he could remember quotations and Latin derivatives while he left such things as anagrams to me. As he had always read books at night I found crosswords filled this gap. The only slight problem was that occasionally he would mix up clues. For example, I would read, 'Was in his turn a Red Indian', which we answered, then after I had read the next clue, 'Something taken for granted', he would repeat it as, 'Was in turn taken for granted'. Apart from this though, his ability to solve the clues has increased and he now

TS-H

109

enjoys telling me that his memory is better than mine—with which I agree!

Friends who visited, telephoned or invited him to their homes contributed greatly to overcome not only boredom, but his feeling of no longer being a social asset. He was especially happy playing with a friend's dogs and with his grandchildren, who obviously enjoyed his company. For my part I was very grateful to those friends who looked after him when I had to leave him for a few hours. I was too nervous to leave him on his own as if he hurt himself, failed to find something he wanted, or dropped something he thought might damage the carpet, he would panic and shout for my help.

To feel wanted and useful was his crying need and the biggest step forward for him in this direction was when he was referred to "the research world", where it was made clear to him that he could help their research while they tried to help him. At last he felt he could do something which others could not do and he was always eager for the visits or to go on the trips to various hospitals and colleges which were arranged.

The homework reading tests they and their colleagues set showed that, if he tried hard and took his time, he could read more than the newspaper headlines. Although they showed little improvement in the speed of reading, it was the incentive he needed and today he reads short passages for pleasure but still too slowly for him to follow the story of a book or a long article. Apart from the enjoyment of doing them, it was difficult for me to judge how much benefit he obtained from the many other tests he was given.

I had to take charge of the pills he had to have each day, as he could never remember if he had taken them, even from the beginning to the end of a meal. One radio had to remain tuned to his favourite station and a piece of white adhesive tape fixed to the 'on' button of both the radio and the T.V. He used the radio a lot, but seldom bothered with the T.V. unless I was there to explain which tennis player was hitting the ball or what animal was on the screen etc. He did not look at or listen to plays, as he could not remember the story and only recognised the voices of the characters who appeared frequently, such as those in Coronation Street.

Looking for ways to help me in the garden, he decided to tidy the orchard where he knew there were no flowers to confuse him. This seemed a good idea, and John started to mow the lawn. However he got stung by nettles which he grasped thinking they were long grass. I watched from the window as he went several times over the same place and missed other areas. In the end I would walk in front of the mower to show him where to go—a practice of which we soon both tired! Other efforts excited him to exhibitions of frustration, as flowers, weeds, and leaves all look the same to him now. We both realised that we would have to move to somewhere without a garden.

Probably his biggest problem was the inability to recognise things or people by sight. This I thought could be improved by logical reasoning. For example, when looking for his spectacles he would not think where he had used them last but rather looked in the most unlikely places, eventually asking me to find them. He disliked being in crowds, so when shopping he would wait for me outside the shop. I suggested he might recognise me by my height, spectacles, shape of coat, shoes, and handbag but he never spots me and I always have to call him. Once he thought he was being very clever and began helping to unload a trolley at the check out, much to the surprise of a lady who must have been mystified by his apology—'I'm sorry, I thought you were my wife.' He could never tell me where to find an answer to a business problem, kept in the files at home, and he did not appear to be able to work out where the information would be found. While his long-term memory of words he had read or spoken seemed normal, there appeared to be no pictorial memory of places he had seen or the position of papers, clothes, china, etc."

The Move to a Small Flat

"The day eventually came when facts had to be faced. It was obvious that John would not be able to work for some months, if ever. His employers eventually had to terminate his employment, though they had treated us extremely fairly. However, John had shown little improvement in finding his way in the street beyond the limit of about 100 yards, and there were no shops near the house. I could not foresee how he could ever manage by himself. Also we could not afford to maintain the house, so it had to be sold. We discussed the move and John stipulated that the small flat or house should be on the level, near to some small local shops and a post box, and not too far from our local friends. We found such a flat and the packing up started. This was a traumatic experience for me, as anyone who has had to move from a house with a cellar and roof storage to a two-bedroomed flat with no storage space will testify. There was an additional irksome task as John could not recognise his possessions, so I had to be there to sort them out. Once installed in the flat, a re-education programme began and it took some days before he learned to take plates from the dining room into the kitchen and not into the bathroom. Each day I walked with him to the shops, about 100 yards away, where there was also a post box. After several weeks he agreed to post a letter by himself, and watching from the window, I saw him go straight on instead of turning left. Surely, I thought, he will realise his mistake and turn back, but after some minutes I went in search of the lost wanderer. After two years he can be relied on to find his way to the shops where the staff know about his visual agnosia and will help him by collecting the items on a list. If, however, he is asked to find his way home from a road on the opposite side to the flats he gets lost and is usually surprised when I turn into the drive after returning from a car drive.

At first journeys were unpleasant for both of us, as he could not judge speed or distance or read road signs, so when driving at a gentle 40 m.p.h. on a dual carriage way I would be told not to drive so fast and in traffic he would imagine cars were going to hit us. Today I know that he does not enjoy car trips but he has learned to control his fear and to trust the driver. I have learned that, having a passenger who does not map or sign read, and who gets into a frustrated temper if we lose the way, it is better to stick mainly to routes I know."

After Five Years

"We have now worked out a happy partnership with both of us accepting what we can and cannot do. John does some dusting and vacuum cleaning fairly well, but as he tends to dust some items twice and others not at all, I take over when visitors are expected. He opens the garage door, carries the shopping, posts letters, makes the tea and as long as I leave the bottle in the right place, pours himself a glass of sherry. When we have guests I have to pour the drinks otherwise they may not get what they expect!

If there is a beautiful sunset I try and paint a word picture for him so he can join in my pleasure. Similarly I have to describe floral arrangements and the colour of the shirt and tie I have selected for him to wear. This colour problem creates difficulties as, if I relax my vigilance, he uses a dirty white handkerchief or wears odd socks, but his sense of touch has improved so that socks are no longer inside out. I still question his reasoning power. For example, he saw a dog swimming in a river and asked if it was a swan—had he said an otter I would not have been surprised. He has sometimes taken my raincoat from the cupboard instead of his own, not apparently working out that the buttons were on the wrong side. Possibly such lapses are due to lack of concentration as I know he has to think what he is doing all the time. When taking the rubbish to the dustbin, a job I do without thinking, he has to say to himself 'left outside the front door.' Although he leaves business matters to me, he likes to know about them so all letters are read to him and he makes comments and suggestions. His dependence on me to take him for walks, to drive the car, tell him what clothes to wear, arrange our daily programme, etc., must be very frustrating to him. I admit it is a harder job than I had expected to do in my old age, but it has its compensations. Had things been different I should never have met some very interesting, kind, caring and clever medical and scientific people, who have given me great support, help and friendship. Neither should I have had the opportuniy of seeing some fascinating machines in operation or watching research workers at work.

We are lucky to have family and friends with whom we exchange visits. We try and avoid parties as John does not like crowded rooms where noise prevents him hearing other people's voices and he has to ask me to steer him towards people to whom he wishes to speak. At meals he is always seated next to a kind person who can stop him eating the shells of prawns, the lemon at the side of the fish or putting salt instead of sugar on his strawberries. It is to his credit that, in spite of his problem, he has always remained his cheerful self, never moaning, and if he sometimes loses his temper, then who wouldn't?"

References

Adler, A. (1944). Disintegration and restoration of optic recognition in visual agnosia. *Archives of Neurology and Psychiatry, 51,* 243–259.

Adler, A. (1950). Course and outcome of visual agnosia. *Journal of Nervous and Mental Diseases, 111,* 41–51.

Albert, M. L., Reches, D., & Silverberg, R. (1975). Associative visual agnosia without alexia. *Neurology, 25,* 322–326.

Assal, G., Favre, C., & Anderes, J. P. (1984). Non-reconnaissance d'animaux familiers chez un paysan. *Revue Neurologique, 140,* 580–584.

Baddeley, A. D. (1979). Working memory and reading. In P. A. Kolers, M. E. Wrolstad, & H. Bouma (Eds.), *Processing of visible language* (Vol. 1). New York: Plenum Press.

Bálint, R. (1909). Seelenlahmung des "Schauens": Optische ataxie, raumliche Störung der Aufmerksamkeit. *Monatschrift für Psychiatrie und Neurologie, 25,* 51–81.

Bay, E. (1950). Agnosie und Funktionswandel. *Monograph Gesamtgeben Neurologie und Psychiatrie, 73,* 1–94. Berlin: Springer.

Bay, E. (1953). Disturbances of visual perception and their examination. *Brain, 76,* 515–551.

Beauvois, M. F. (1982). Optic aphasia: A process of interaction between vision and language. *Philosophical Transactions of the Royal Society, London, B 298,* 35–47.

Beauvois, M. F. & Saillant, B. (1985). Optic aphasia for colours and colour agnosia: A distinction between visual and visuo-verbal impairments in the processing of colours. *Cognitive Neuropsychology, 2,* 1–48.

Bender, M. B. & Feldman, M. (1972). The so-called "visual agnosias". *Brain, 95,* 173–186.

Benson, D. F. & Greenberg, J. P. (1969). Visual form agnosia. *Archives of Neurology, 20,* 82–89.

Beyn, E. S. & Knyazeva, G. R. (1962). The problem of prosopagnosia. *Journal of Neurology, Neurosurgery and Psychiatry, 25,* 154–158.

Bornstein, B. & Kidron, D. P. (1959). Prosopagnosia. *Journal of Neurology, Neurosurgery and Psychiatry, 22,* 124–131.

Bornstein, B., Sroka, H., & Munitz, H. (1969). Prosopagnosia with animal face agnosia. *Cortex, 5,* 164–169.

Bromley, J. M., Humphreys, G. W., Javadnia, A., Riddoch, M. J., & Ruddock, K. H. (1986). Pattern discrimination in a human subject suffering visual agnosia. *Journal of Physiology*, *377*, 67p.

Campion, J. (in press). Apperceptive agnosia: The specification of constructs and their use. In G. W. Humphreys & M. J. Riddoch (Eds.), *Visual object processing: A cognitive neuropsychological approach*. London: Lawrence Erlbaum Associates.

Campion, J. & Latto, R. (1985). Apperceptive agnosia due to carbon monoxide poisoning: An interpretation based on critical band masking from disseminated lesions. *Behavioural Brain Research*, *15*, 227–240.

Charcot, J. M. (1883). Un cas de suppression brusque et isolee de la vision mentale des signes et des objects (formes et coleurs). *Progress Medicale*, *11*, 568–571.

Coltheart, M., Patterson, K. E., & Marshall, J. C. (Eds.) (1980). *Deep dyslexia*. London: Routledge and Kegan Paul.

Cowey, A. (1979). Cortical maps and visual perception: The Grindley memorial lecture. *Quarterly Journal of Experimental Psychology*, *31*, 1–17.

Cowey, A. (1985). Aspects of cortical organization related to attention and selective impairments of visual perception: A tutorial review. In M. I. Posner & O. S. M. Marin (Eds.), *Attention and performance XI*. Hillsdale, N.J.: Lawrence Erlbaum Associates.

Critchley, M. (1964). The problem of visual agnosia. *Journal of Neurological Science*, *1*, 274–290.

Damasio, A. R., Damasio, H., & Van Hoesen G. W. (1982). Prosopagnosia: Anatomic basis and behavioral mechanisms. *Neurology*, *32*, 331–341.

Danta, G., Hilton, R. C., & O'Boyle, D. J. (1978). Hemisphere function and binocular depth perception. *Brain*, *101*, 569–589.

Davidoff, J. & Wilson, B. (1985). A case of visual agnosia showing a disorder of pre-semantic vision classification. *Cortex*, *21*, 121–134.

Ettlinger, G. & Wyke, M. (1961). Defects in identifying objects visually in a patient with cerebrovascular disease. *Journal of Neurology, Neurosurgery and Psychiatry*, *24*, 254–259.

Fischer, B. & Poggio, G. F. (1979). Depth sensitivity of binocular cortical neurons of behaving monkeys. *Proceedings of the Royal Society, London, B 204*, 409–414.

Frisby, J. (1979). *Seeing*. Oxford: Oxford University Press.

Goldstein, K. & Gelb, A. (1918). Psychologische analysen hirnpathologischer Fall auf Grund von Untersuchungen Hirnveletzter. *Zeitschrift für die gesemete Neurologie und Psychiatrie*, *41*, 1–142.

Gomori, A. J. & Hawryluk, G. A. (1984). Visual agnosia without alexia. *Neurology*, *34*, 947–950.

Gregory, R. (1970). *The intelligent eye*. London: Weidenfield and Nicholson.

Hécaen, H. (1981). Neuropsychology of face recognition. In G. Davies, H. Ellis, & J. Shepherd (Eds.), *Perceiving and remembering faces*. London: Academic Press.

Hillyard, S. A., & Munte, T. F. (1984). Selective attention to color and locational cues: An analysis with event-related brain potentials. *Perception & Psychophysics*, *36*, 185–198.

Hochberg, J. (1968). In the mind's eye. In R. N. Haber (Ed.), *Contemporary theory and research in visual perception*. New York: Holt Rinehart and Winston.

Hochberg, J. (1978). *Perception*. Englewood Cliffs, N.J.: Prentice-Hall.

Holmes, G. (1918). Disturbances of vision by cerebral lesions. *British Journal of Ophthalmology*, *2*, 353–384.

Hubel, D. H., & Wiesel, T. N. (1962). Receptive fields, binocular interaction and functional architecture in the cat's visual cortex. *Journal of Physiology*, *160*, 106–154.

Hubel, D. H., & Wiesel, T. N. (1968). Receptive fields and functional architecture in the cat's visual cortex. *Journal of Physiology*, *166*, 106–154.

Humphreys, G. W. (1981). Flexibility of attention between stimulus dimensions. *Perception & Psychophysics, 30*, 291–302.

Humphreys, G. W. & Riddoch, M. J. (1984). Routes to object constancy: Implications for neurological impairments of object constancy. *Quarterly Journal of Experimental Psychology, 36A*, 385–415. (See also the author's correction, *Quarterly Journal of Experimental Psychology*, 1985, *37A*, 493–495.)

Humphreys, G. W. & Riddoch, M. J. (Eds.). (in press/a). *Visual object processing: A cognitive neuropsychological approach*. London: Lawrence Erlbaum Associates.

Humphreys, G. W. & Riddoch, M. J. (in press/b). The fractionation of visual agnosia. In G. W. Humphreys & M. J. Riddoch (Eds.), *Visual object processing: A cognitive neuropsychological approach*. London: Lawrence Erlbaum Associates.

Humphreys, G. W., Riddoch, M. J., & Quinlan, P. T. (1985). Interactive processes in perceptual organization: Evidence from visual agnosia. In M. I. Posner & O. S. M. Marin (Eds.), Attention & performance XI. Hillsdale, N.J.: Lawrence Erlbaum Associates.

Johansson, G. (1973). Visual perception of biological motion and a model for its analysis. *Perception & Psychophysics, 14*, 201–211.

Johansson, G. (1975). Visual motion perception. *Scientific American, 232*, 76–88.

Julesz, B. (1971). *Foundations of cyclopean perception*. Chicago: University of Chicago Press.

Kertesz, A. (1979). Visual agnosia: The dual deficit of perception and recognition. *Cortex, 15*, 403–419.

Levine, D. (1978). Prosopagnosia and visual object agnosia: A behavioural study. *Brain and Language, 5*, 351–365.

Lissauer, H. (1890). Ein Fall von Seelenblindheit nebst einem Beitrage zur Theorie derselben. *Archiv für Psychiatrie und Nervenkrankheiten, 21*, 222–270.

Luria, A. R. (1973). *The working brain*. London: Penguin Books.

Mack, J. L. & Boller, F. (1977). Associative visual agnosia and its related deficits: The role of the minor hemisphere in assigning meaning to visual perceptions: *Neuropsychologia, 15*, 345–351.

Macrae, D. & Trolle, E. (1956). The defect of function in visual agnosia. *Brain, 79*, 94–110.

Marin, O. S. M. (in press). Dementia and visual agnosia. In G. W. Humphreys & M. J. Riddoch (Eds.), *Visual object processing: A cognitive neuropsychological approach*. London: Lawrence Erlbaum Associates.

Marr, D. (1976). Early processing of visual information. *Philosophical Transactions of the Royal Society, London, B 275*, 483–524.

Marr, D. (1980). Visual information processing: The structure and creation of visual representations. *Philosophical Transactions of the Royal Society, London, B 290*, 199–218.

Marr, D. (1982). *Vision*. San Francisco: W. H. Freeman.

Marr, D. & Hildreth, E. (1980). Theory of edge detection. *Proceedings of the Royal Society, London, B 207*, 187–217.

Marr, D. & Nishihara, H. K. (1978). Representation and recognition of the spatial organization of three-dimensional shapes. *Proceedings of the Royal Society, London, B 200*, 269–294.

Meadows, J. C. (1974). Disturbed perception of colours associated with localised cerebral lesions. *Brain, 97*, 615–632.

Mollon, J. D., Newcombe, F., Polden, P. G., & Ratcliff, G. (1980). On the presence of the three cone mechanisms in a case of total achromatopsia. In G. Verriest (Ed.), *Colour vision deficiences* (Vol. 5). Bristol: Hilger.

Munk, H. (1881). *Ueber die Funktionen der Grosshirnrinde*. Gesammelte Mitteilungen aus den Jahren 1877–1880. Berlin: Hirschwald.

Newcombe, F. & Ratcliff, G. (1975). Agnosia: A disorder of object recognition. In F. Michel & B. Schott (Eds.), *Les syndromes de disconnexion calleuse chez l'homme*. Lyon: Colloque International.

Nielsen, J. M. (1946). *Agnosia, apraxia, aphasia: Their value in cerebral localization* (2nd edition). New York: Hoeber.

Pallis, C. A. (1955). Impaired identification of faces and places with agnosia for colours. *Journal of Neurology, Neurosurgery and Psychiatry, 18*, 218–224.

Palmer, S. E. (1975a). Visual perception and world knowledge: Notes on a model of sensory-cognitive interaction. In D. A. Norman, D. E. Rumelhart and the LNR Research Group (Eds.), *Explorations in cognition*. San Francisco: W. H. Freeman.

Palmer, S. E. (1975b). The effects of contextual scenes on the identification of objects. *Memory and Cognition, 3*, 519–526.

Pavlov, I. P. (1927). *Conditioned reflexes: An investigation of the physiological activity of the cerebral cortex* (Translated by G. V. Anrep). London: Oxford University Press.

Perret, D. I., Smith, P. A. J., Potter, D. D., Mistlin, A. J., Head, A. S., Milner, A. D., & Jeeves, M. (1985). Visual cells in the temporal cortex sensitive to face view and gaze direction. *Proceedings of the Royal Society, London, B 223*, 293–317.

Posner, M. I. (1969). Abstraction and the process of recognition. In J. T. Spence & G. Bower (Eds.), *The psychology of learning and motivation* (Vol. 3). New York: Academic Press.

Plum, F., Posner, J., & Hain, R. F. (1962). Delayed neurological deterioration after anoxia. *Archives of International Medicine, 110*, 18–25.

Ratcliff, G. (1985). *Agnosia and internal representations: Some second thoughts*. Paper presented to the Cognitive Neuropsychology meeting, Venice.

Ratcliff, G. & Newcombe, F. (1982). Object recognition: Some deductions from the clinical evidence. In A. W. Ellis (Ed.), *Normality and pathology in cognitive functions*. London: Academic Press.

Richardson, J. C., Chambers, R. A., & Heywood, P. M. (1959). Encephalopathies of anoxia and hypoglycemia. *Archives of Neurology, 1*, 178–190.

Riddoch, G. (1917). Dissociation of visual perceptions due to occipital injuries, with especial reference to appreciation of movement. *Brain, 40*, 15–57.

Riddoch, M. J. & Humphreys, G. W. (1986). Neurological impairments of object constancy: The effects of orientation and size disparities. *Cognitive Neuropsychology, 3*, 207–224.

Riddoch, M. J. & Humphreys, G. W. (in press/a). A case of integrative visual agnosia. *Brain*.

Riddoch, M. J. & Humphreys, G. W. (in press/b). Visual agnosia: Anatomical and functional accounts. In F. Clifford-Rose & C. Kennard (Eds.), *Physiological aspects of clinical neuro-opthalmology*. London: Chapman Hall. Mansell Bequest symposium.

Riddoch, M. J. & Humphreys, G. W. (in press/c). Visual object processing in optic aphasia: A case of semantic access agnosia. *Cognitive Neuropsychology*.

Robinson, J. O. (1972). *The psychology of visual illusion*. New York: Hutchinson.

Rock, I. (1956). The orientation of forms on the retina and in the environment. *The American Journal of Psychology, 69*, 513–528.

Rock, I. (1973). *Orientation and form*. New York: Academic Press.

Rubens, A. D. & Benson, D. F. (1971). Associative visual agnosia. *Archives of Neurology, 24*, 305–316.

Rubin, E. (1915). Synoplevede Figurer. Translated in D. C. Beardslee & M. Westheimer (Eds.), *Readings in perception*. Princeton N.J.: Princeton University Press.

Schweickert, R. & Boruff, B. (1986). Short-term memory capacity: Magic number or magic spell. *Journal of Experimental Psychology: Learning, Memory and Cognition, 12*, 419–425.

Sergent, J. (in press). Information processing and laterality effects: Implications for object and face perception. In G. W. Humphreys & M. J. Riddoch (Eds.), *Visual object processing: A cognitive neuropsychological approach*. London: Lawrence Erlbaum Associates.

Shallice, T. & Warrington, E. K. (1980). Single and multiple component central dyslexic syndromes. In M. Coltheart, K. E. Patterson, & J. C. Marshall (Eds.), *Deep dyslexia.* London: Routledge and Kegan Paul.

Shallice, T., Warrington, E. K., & McCarthy, R. (1983). Reading without semantics. *Quarterly Journal of Experimental Psychology, 27,* 187–199.

Snodgrass, J. G. & Vanderwart, M. A. (1980). Standardized set of 260 pictures: Norms for name agreement, image agreement, familiarity and visual complexity. *Journal of Experimental Psychology: Human Learning and Memory, 6,* 174–215.

Taylor, A. & Warrington, E. K. (1971). Visual agnosia: A single case report. *Cortex, 7,* 152–161.

Tusa, R. J., Palmer, L. A., & Rosenquist, A. C. (1975). The retinotopic organization of the visual cortex in the cat. *Neuroscience Abstracts, 1,* 52.

Ungerleider, L. G. (1985). The corticocortical pathways for object recognition and spatial perception. In C. Chagas (Ed.), *Pattern recognition mechanisms.* Pontificae Academiae Scientiarum Scripta Varia

Van Essen, D. C. (1985). Functional organization of primate visual cortex. In A. Peters & E. G. Jones (Eds.), *Cerebral cortex, (Vol. 3): Visual Cortex.* New York: Plenum Press.

Volkmann, F. C. (1976). Saccadic suppression: A brief review. In R. A. Monty & J. W. Senders (Eds.), *Eye movements and psychological processes.* Hillsdale, N.J.: Lawrence Erlbaum Associates.

Walls, G. L. (1942). *The vertebrate eye and its adaptive radiation.* Cranbrook: Cranbrook Institute of Science.

Wapner, W., Judd, T., & Gardner, H. (1978). Visual agnosia in an artist. *Cortex, 14,* 343–364.

Warrington, E. K. (1982). Neuropsychological studies of object recognition. *Philosophical Transactions of the Royal Society, London, B 298,* 15–33.

Warrington, E. K. (1985). Agnosia: The impairment of object recognition. In J. A. M. Frederiks (Ed.), *Handbook of clinical neurology (Vol. 1): Clinical neuropsychology.* Amsterdam: Elsevier Science.

Warrington, E. K., & Shallice, T. (1984). Category specific semantic impairments. *Brain, 107,* 829–854.

Warrington, E. K., & Taylor, A. (1973). The contribution of the right parietal lobe to object recognition *Cortex, 9,* 152 164.

Warrington, E. K., & Taylor, A. (1978). Two categorical stages of object recognition. *Perception, 7,* 695–705.

Weller, R. E. & Kaas, J. H. (1985). Cortical projections of the dorsolateral visual area in owl monkeys: The prestriate relay to inferotemporal cortex. *Journal of Comparative Neurology, 234,* 35–59.

Zeki, S. M. (1974). Cells responding to changing image and size and disparity in the cortex of the rhesus monkey. *Journal of Physiology, 243,* 827–841.

Zeki, S. M. (1978). Functional specialization in the visual cortex of the rhesus monkey. *Nature, 274,* 423–428.

Zeki, S. M. (1980). The representation of colours in the cerebral cortex. *Nature, 284,* 412–418.

Zihl, J., Von Cramon, D., & Mai, N. (1983). Selective disturbance of movement vision after bilateral brain damage. *Brain, 106,* 313–340.

Author Index

Subject Index